The Meaning ❦ of the ❦ Constitution

The Meaning of the Constitution

ANGELA RODDEY HOLDER, LL.M.

MEMBER OF THE BARS OF CONNECTICUT, SOUTH CAROLINA, AND LOUISIANA

FORMERLY, DEPARTMENT OF POLITICAL SCIENCE
WINTHROP COLLEGE
COUNSEL FOR MEDICOLEGAL AFFAIRS
YALE UNIVERSITY SCHOOL OF MEDICINE
AND
YALE-NEW HAVEN HOSPITAL
AND
CLINICAL PROFESSOR OF PEDIATRICS (LAW)
WITH
JOHN W. LEWIS, M.D., F.A.C.S., J.D.
AND
POLLY PHILBROOK LEWIS, J.D.
AND
MELFORD A. WILSON, PH.D.

FOREWORD BY HENRY STEELE COMMAGER

SECOND EDITION

BARRON'S
EDUCATIONAL SERIES, INC.
New York / London / Toronto / Sydney

All inquiries should be addressed to:
Barron's Educational Series, Inc.
250 Wireless Blvd.
Hauppauge, NY 11788

Library of Congress Catalog Card No. 87-1852

International Standard Book No. 0-8120-3847-9

Library of Congress Cataloging-in-Publication Data

Holder, Angela Roddey.
  The meaning of the Constitution.

  Bibliography: p. 119
  Includes index.
  1. United States—Constitutional law. I. Lewis,
John W. (John Walter) II. Lewis, Polly Philbrook.
III. Title.
KF4550.Z9H6 1987   342.73′023   87-1852
ISBN 0-8120-3847-9   347.30223

Printed in the United States of America

90   510   9 8 7 6 5 4 3

For John

with many thanks to David,

the lawyer's lawyer

Contents

CONTENTS

JUSTITIA EST CONSTANS
ET PERPETUA VOLUNTAS JUS
SUUM CUIQUE TRIBUENDI

Foreword

IN THE FIRST OF THE FEDERALIST PAPERS, Alexander Hamilton wrote that

> It has been frequently remarked that it seems to have been reserved to the people of this country, by their conduct and example, to decide the important question whether societies of men are really capable or not of establishing good government from reflection and choice, or whether they are forever destined to depend for their political constitutions on accident and force.

The government they did establish, "by reflection and choice," was the first of written national constitutions, the first to be made by "we the people," the first to inaugurate a federal system that worked, the first to embrace a Bill of Rights that was not merely procedural, the first to separate formally Church and State, the first to expand not by "colonies" but by admitting new settlements as coordinated States. It was the first, too, to create an independent judiciary and to prescribe "judicial review" of legislation binding on State and Nation alike.

Thus, from the beginnings of our national history, the courts undertook the task of expounding not only the Law but also the Constitution itself, until eventually it came to be pretty generally accepted that, as Chief Justice Hughes once said, "the Constitution is what the Judges say it is." American courts, unlike those of other nations, were expected to preside over litigation, work out solutions in conflict of laws, umpire the Federal system, rule on international law, prescribe the bounds of both State and Federal authority and of the popular will, and educate a hetero geneous people to the most complicated government ever devised by the ingenuity of man. Thanks to the wisdom of the Framers, the Judges assigned these heavy responsibilities were immunized from the most dangerous buffetings of popular opinion and politics. Because the courts played so crucial a role, Presidents and Senators have pretty consistently avoided partisanship in appointments, and thus have attracted to the Bench men of the highest talent and integrity. If we have an aristocracy in America, it is, as de Tocqueville observed 150 years ago, "the aristocracy of the robe." At the very beginnings of our judicial history, American courts adopted the habit of elaborate written opinions, of seriatim opinions and, a practice all but unknown elsewhere, of dissenting opinions. These were, in effect, appeals from the present to the future, but courts were not invariably dependent on precedent. They could override earlier decisions in order to accommodate the Constitution to the necessities of the time—thus making sure it would be a living instrument. With infinite patience, they accorded to every case and every plaintiff the most scrupulous attention and the ripest wisdom. Over the years—almost two centuries—they have built up, case by case, the most imposing body of constitutional law known to history. If we confine ourselves to secular literature, we can say with confidence that nothing compares with this affluent enterprise. When we contemplate this record, we can say, with Justice Holmes, that "our eyes dazzle."

****

Students are fortunate to have for their guidance Professor Holder's book *The Meaning of the Constitution*. It is concise but comprehensive. Notable for its clarity of statement, its accuracy of summation and of clause-by-clause explanation—almost word-by-word—it provides, at almost every level, the essentials for understanding not only the significance of the words and clauses of the Constitution, but also the adjudication of these words and clauses. Its selection of key cases is at once catholic and discriminating. It provides, too, an admirable working bibliography. Finally, it is aware of the changing meaning of such terms as "equal protection of the laws," "regulation of commerce," or "establishment of religion." In all this, it observes a nice impartiality. I know of no other handbook that will prove as useful and sound as *The Meaning of the Constitution*.

HENRY STEELE COMMAGER

Preface

THE CONSTITUTION OF THE UNITED STATES exists to provide a system within which our nation can solve its problems. It is as relevant in determining the legality of aid to the Nicaraguan Contras as it was when President Jefferson dealt with the Barbary pirates. For each generation of Americans, our problems may seem different from what has gone before, but within our Constitutional system we have sufficient flexibility to find new solutions. Our belief in the inalienable rights of all people has been absolute. At some points in our history, including today, our execution of that belief has been less than satisfactory, but those principles are the goal toward which our nation strives. Our Constitution on its 200th birthday remains the declaration of this nation's commitment to the dignity and worth of every person.

Before any generation can solve its problems, it must understand the system within which it exists and what resources for problem-solving are available. I hope this book explains our system in such a way that the reader understands his or her rights and, more important, his or her responsibilities.

Yale University School of Medicine   ANGELA RODDEY HOLDER
March, 1987

Introduction

THE RATIFICATION OF THE 26TH AMENDMENT in 1971 meant that most of the readers of this book are eligible to vote. The right to vote means the right to participate in the selection of the people who make policies which affect the lives not only of everyone in this country, including the voter, but of most of the other people in the world.

The Amendment giving eighteen year olds the right to vote was proposed and ratified because at the time, those who were too young to vote for the people who made American foreign policy were not too young to be drafted and to die in Viet Nam. Student unrest in the 1960's and early 1970's changed the foreign policy of this country.

The 1980's have seen a trend away from political activities among young citizens, but today their influence is needed more than ever. Issues such as disarmament, environmental pollution and poverty will affect not only our lives but the lives of our children and grandchildren. Those segments of the population who do not vote are usually ignored when political decisions are made. I hope that the students who read this book will realize the importance of political participation, not only for yourselves as individuals but for the society whose interests you can express.

The Background of the Constitution

POLITICAL PHILOSOPHY had its beginnings in ancient Greece, where Aristotle, in particular, believed in a concept of "absolute justice." He believed in natural law arising from man's power to reason and, through reason, his ability to determine what justice was and to apply it. Absolute justice could never be attained in practice, but it remained the ideal by which men could measure the ethics of their relationships with others, just as the life of Christ remains the unattainable standard by which Christians of today judge their own conduct. Aristotle believed that men throughout the world would, through reason, arrive at the same views on the nature of universal justice just as the idea of "fire" is the same everywhere, but because local conditions varied, the practice of justice would vary, just as a man in Greece and a man in Persia would think of very different things if they thought of "money."

In the 13th Century, St. Thomas Aquinas wrote *Summa Theologica* in which he followed Aristotle's idea of the existence of natural law and absolute justice, but Aquinas believed that they were derived from God. He defined natural law as that portion of the eternal and divine law of God which man could discover by the use of his power to reason. Aquinas believed that natural law governed the relationships among men or between men and the state in somewhat the same way that the physical laws of God regulate the planets. Each man's conscience was a gift of God enabling him to determine the difference between good and evil, and this faculty of the human spirit decided what was or was not in keeping with natural law.

Aquinas believed that God instituted governments to meet the needs of mankind and that the state originated in His will. The state was obliged to comply with the will of God and natural law in the same manner as the individual. If the state made laws which contravened a man's conscience, he was theoretically not bound by them, but Aquinas believed that the unjust ruler would receive his punishment in the hereafter and that it was not the business of the citizen to overthrow a tyrant. Disturbance was to be avoided at all cost, even that of injustice, and obedience was more important than liberty.

By the 17th Century, Aquinas' ideas, which had been of profound importance in governmental theory for centuries, had developed into the idea that the king rules by Divine Right. Regardless of how unfair he might be, a rebellion against him was considered to be a rebellion against God, Who, it was thought, had established that particular king on that particular throne.

In 1689 John Locke, an English philosopher, wrote his *Second Treatise on Civil Government* to justify the English Revolution of the year before, to reject the idea of the "Divine Right of Kings," and to dispute Aquinas' view of the origin of the state. Locke's ideas were the basis of the philosophical justification for the American Revolution and his concept of the rights of man are basic to the Constitution.

Locke agreed with Aquinas that there was something known as "natural law" although he was much less positive about its source. To Locke, natural law meant that men, because of their humanity, have certain inalienable rights which should not be transgressed by the state or other men, and that among these inalienable rights are the right to life, liberty and property. Our Declaration of Independence expresses these ideas of Locke's when it states: "We hold these truths to be self-evident, that all men are created equal, that they are endowed by their Creator with certain unalienable rights, that among these are Life, Liberty and the pursuit of Happiness."

In this sense, natural law and the natural rights which arise from it are still a part of our law. In 1952, for example, the United States Supreme Court held that a policeman who held a suspect down and forcibly pumped his stomach to obtain evidence had violated the suspect's Constitutional rights so flagrantly that he had disregarded the principles of "a sense of justice and the requirements of certain decencies of civilized conduct." [1] In 1965 the Court held that a husband and wife have a basic right to privacy in their marital relations.[2] While the Court denies that it rests its decisions on some abstract theory of natural law, it has frequently pointed out that our basic and inalienable rights as listed in the Bill of Rights must be protected and occasionally finds new "natural rights" it deems worthy of protection.

In modern times most countries have such highly developed codes of laws that reliance on abstract natural law alone as a basis for judicial procedure is most unusual. However, the 1962 trial of Adolf Eichmann was entirely the product of natural law. Eichmann, a leader in the Nazi extermination of the Jews, was tried in Israel for his crimes during World War II. At the time he committed his atrocities, there was no state of Israel and consequently no Israeli law. There is a principle of criminal law in all parts of the civilized world that a man should not be tried for something not specifically prohibited by a statute in force at the time he did it. In the Eichmann case, however, there was a consensus among legal experts that natural law and civilized behavior prohibit the extermination of millions of people, and so Eichmann was tried, convicted and executed under natural law.

Where Locke and Aquinas most strongly disagreed, and where our political philosophy followed Locke, was in the concept of the origin of the state. Locke believed that the source of political power was derived from the people and not, as Aquinas did, that it was imposed from above. In his *Second Treatise on Civil Government,* Locke wrote an allegory about the origin of the state and its government in which he began with a pre-political society, very similar to life in the Garden of Eden. In this society, there were no laws, no rulers, and no government and everyone was quite satisfied with his lot. This society was governed entirely by reason—as Aristotle and Aquinas had also thought that men were governed by reason—and no one was so unreasonable as to interfere with another person. However, a few citizens transgressed others' rights and it became *convenient* to establish some rules and regulations—in other words, a government. The government was established solely for the sake of convenience to permit everyone to live together with a minimum of strife and not, as Aquinas believed, because God willed it. This was called the "social contract" theory because the citizens made a promise or contract to abide by the rules to protect themselves. The basis of Locke's idea was that government existed only by the consent of the governed.

In 1620 the Pilgrims wrote and signed the Mayflower Compact before they landed at Plymouth Rock. This agreement, signed by all of the men (but none of the women) on the ship, set up a government and made rules under which the colony would live. This is Locke's "social contract" theory in action.

Under this theory, the only reason the government exists is to preserve the life, liberty and property of the citizens and it has no power except that which is used for the good of the people. The basic rights of the people, therefore, limit the power of the ruler, who has no right, Divine or otherwise, to interfere with them. Locke's conclusion was that if the government breaks the trust of the people who established it or if it interferes with the liberty of the citizens, they have a right to rebel and make a new contract under which they may govern themselves more conveniently. This right to rebel was the theory behind our Declaration of Independence, which declared that the colonies found government under the King of England to be highly inconvenient as well as detrimental to their liberties.

Our history as an independent nation began on July 4, 1776, when the Declaration of Independence was signed by representatives of the thirteen colonies. At this point, although we declared ourselves free of English rule, there was, of course, no system of national government, so the Second Continental Congress assembled to form one.

The Congress elected a committee of twelve men to draw up a system of government and this committee wrote the Articles of Confederation. The Articles were presented to Congress in 1777 and ratified by all the states except Maryland in 1778 and 1779. Since the colonists' objections to the English King had centered around his use of arbitrary power, they were convinced that a strong central government would soon be guilty of the same abuses. The Articles were, therefore, written with the idea of restricting the power of the national government as much as possible and of forming a league of states which would work together as separate entities.

Under the Articles, the national government was virtually powerless. There was no Executive Branch of the government, although there was a President of the Congress, and consequently no one to enforce the laws which Congress passed. The states could and did ignore any national laws which did not suit them. The national government could only request the states to send money, troops and supplies to fight the Revolution.

Internal difficulties, such as the competing currencies issued by seven different states, made it obvious that the Articles were in need of revision. A conference was called at Mount Vernon in 1786 and another one in Annapolis, Maryland, without substantial improvement. Finally, in 1787 what was to become the Constitutional Convention met in Philadelphia in secret session to decide what to do. They knew that they had to create a system of government in which the national authority would be sufficient to minister to the needs of the nation. The convention had been called to revise the Articles of Confederation, but once the delegates were assembled, they agreed that the same principle of the "right to rebel" which had been invoked against the King would again apply, and since the government established by the Articles was no longer suited to the convenience of the people, they would create another one. They wrote our Constitution and developed the system of government under which we have lived for almost 200 years.

The Constitution in Our History

OUR SYSTEM of government is a great deal more than the words written by the Constitutional Convention and ratified by the people. A constitution is a framework which establishes the basic principles of government and leaves the brushstrokes and details to the institutions it creates. At the time the new government began in 1789, it operated under a document which asked more questions than it answered. It provided for "due process of law." What is that? What is "interstate commerce?" As these definitions were supplied, so the government grew. Our Constitution has survived for the very simple reason that its flexibility and lack of detail have permitted it to change with new patterns of living and new standards of justice and morality as they are accepted by the people. There are those who feel that the Constitution should be interpreted today as it was in 1789, but had it not been allowed to grow and change while preserving our governmental structure, it would long ago have been unworkable and as doomed to dust as the Articles of Confederation. Our Constitution today is the basic authority for federal and state laws which regulate air transportation, television stations, public education, space exploration, generation of electricity, heart transplants and other aspects of our ordinary lives which the Founding Fathers would have considered miracles beyond belief. This capacity to grow with social conditions and technology while preserving the institutional structure of the government has been the Constitution's triumph and success and proves that we do have "a living Constitution."

The Constitution has been amended very few times because most changes which are required in the methods of government are brought about by the passage of ordinary laws or by new interpretations. The meaning of the words to which the delegates at the Constitutional Convention signed their names is determined by action of the three branches of government and by the customs of doing things which have evolved in the course of American history.

Many aspects of our system which we take for granted are not established by law. We just do them in a certain way and as long as customary procedures function satisfactorily, no one seeks to change them. The nominating conventions of both parties grew by trial and error and are not controlled by federal law at all. Political parties themselves were unknown in the early years of the country. The first three presidential candidates were nominated in a very disorganized fashion and after that, candidates were nominated by Congressional caucus. The convention, although unlike those we have today, was invented by the Anti-masonic party in 1832. The use of congressional committees is also based on custom and tradition and is now considered an indispensible part of the legislative process. The president's cabinet is largely governed by tradition and was not created by the Constitution.

The president has enormous influence in interpreting and expanding the Constitution. At the time President William Henry Harrison died and Tyler became president, it was not clear whether a Vice-President who succeeded to the presidency was really president or whether he was an "acting president" empowered only to conduct a holding operation until the next election. Tyler made it clear that he was the President and exercized all the powers of the office, thus establishing the precedent which has been accepted ever since. Thomas Jefferson completed the Louisiana Purchase first and asked for congressional approval afterwards, thus continuing Washington's precedent that although the Senate has the authority to "advise and consent" to treaties, they are first negotiated by the executive without legislative interference. Theodore Roosevelt invented the concept of an "executive agreement" which, like a treaty, involves relations with other nations, but which does not require confirmation by the Senate. Every president since his time has used this power. Presidents in this century commenced the practice of proposing legislation to Congress instead of waiting for Congress to initiate it, and for many years almost all important legislation has been initiated by the White House. Since the time of Washington, presidents have made use of his interpretation of the executive's right as Commander-in-Chief to include the right to dispatch troops at home or abroad without waiting for a congressional declaration of war. The growth through interpretation of presidential power is one of the more obvious ways in which our governmental framework has grown to meet the needs of a growing nation.

Congress has also expanded the Constitution by interpretation. For example, Article I gives Congress the power to "lay and collect taxes." This is a rather meaningless phrase. What kind of taxes? Income taxes? Excise taxes? Sales taxes? What rates will be levied? Will everyone pay the same rate? How will taxes be collected? The constitutional authority behind our system of federal taxation is in four words, but explaining and expanding their meaning requires many volumes devoted to the tax laws passed by Congress. Congress also has the power to "regulate interstate commerce," and this clause has been the authority for more legislation than any other. Under this grant of power and interpretation of what it means, Congress has regulated virtually all labor-management relations, prohibited discrimination by race in business enterprises and prohibited the sale of noxious foods. All these examples serve to show how the meaning of one small phrase has been kept sufficiently flexible to insure that our Constitution serves us as well now in a time of surrogate parents and space flights and other new wonders as it did in the small and rural nation of 1789.

The greatest burden of Constitutional exposition and interpretation, however, has fallen on the judicial branch of the government and particularly on the United States Supreme Court. The history of the Supreme Court is the history of the development of the Constitution and in its decisions can be demonstrated clearly how concepts such as natural rights, freedom, justice, and morality have evolved in a period of 200 years. As Chief Justice Charles Evans Hughes wrote in 1907: "The Constitution is what the Judges say it is."

The Court — 1789-1835

The first great Chief Justice of the Supreme Court was John Marshall of Virginia. He established the Supreme Court as a branch of government equal in power to the other two and, under his leadership, our basic principles of government were enunciated. Until Marshall took office in 1801, the Supreme Court had little power and less prestige. George Washington had several prospective appointees for the Court turn him down, primarily because they believed it too insignificant for their notice. John Jay, the first Chief Justice, resigned to become Governor of New York, a job which he felt to be much more important. Marshall, appointed by John Adams, was the fourth Chief Justice and remained on the Court until his death in 1835. Since he is now accorded a reverent place in American history, it is interesting to note that his appointment narrowly escaped defeat in the Senate.

From 1801 until about 1820, the primary issue in the new nation was the question of the extent of the powers of the federal government. The Founding Fathers had declared that the Constitution was "the supreme law of the land" but they neglected to specify how this idea was to be sustained. The judges of that time were, therefore, very much inclined to place preservation of the young nation high on their list of priorities and to decide cases with that end in view wherever possible. At the time of Marshall's death, that question had been answered, although the Civil War was fought over its practical enforcement.

Marshall's first major case was *Marbury v. Madison*[1] in 1803. Mr. Marbury had been appointed a justice of the peace by President Adams the day before Jefferson's inauguration but had never received his commission, which the new president's staff refused to give to him. Marbury asked the Supreme Court to issue a writ ordering that the commission be delivered, as the Court was allowed to do under the Judiciary Act of 1789. Marshall's opinion denied the writ, thus preventing undue political reaction from President Jefferson, but he declared the Judiciary Act itself, the basis of Marbury's suit, unconstitutional. This decision set the precedent, followed ever since, that when any ordinary law is considered, it must be measured by constitutional standards and if it falls short, it is of no effect. This asserted for the first time that the Constitution, as the foundation of the government, prevails over any ordinary law, state or federal. This further gave the courts the power to be the agents of measurement, thus establishing the principle of "judicial review."

Within four years, Marshall had increased the power of the Court to the point where many congressmen became resentful. An attempt was made to impeach Justice Samuel Chase, primarily because the House did not care for his political views. When the impeachment failed, the principle of judicial independence had been firmly entrenched. Thus was established the now-accepted precept that impeachment will only lie in cases of criminal behavior, not political independence.

The year 1819 saw another major case of Marshall's tenure. The national government owned and controlled a national bank (unlike the "national banks" of today, which are owned by private stockholders and regulated by the government) which was hated by many of the states. The state of Maryland attempted to levy a tax on the bank's assets in Baltimore and the ensuing quarrel went before the Supreme Court as *McCulloch v. Maryland*.[2] This case established two fundamental principles of our legal system. The first objection which the states had to the bank was that the national government had no authority to establish it in the first place. Marshall answered that by declaring the doctrine of "implied powers," which is used today in government subsidy and regulation of all parts of our lives. Marshall declared that the "necessary and proper" clause of Article I, conferring power on the federal government, gave the Congress the power to use *any* convenient means to implement the enumerated powers as long as the means of implementation were not specifically prohibited by the Constitution. This decision meant that although Congress had the power to undertake only those ends for which the Constitution provided, it could use any legal means to achieve them. This decision did more than any other to give the federal government the right to expand its power to meet the challenge of changing times and is probably responsible for the fact that our Constitution has survived our evolution from a small, rural nation to an industrial, urban one. After finding that the bank had been established by implication from the clause giving Congress the power to regulate the credit of the United States, Marshall went on to consider whether Maryland had the power to tax the bank, deciding that it did not. He stated the rule which was to become the cornerstone of our government — that a state government's sovereignty does not extend to actions of the federal government, since the federal government was established by all the people and hence is not subject to attack by a small group of them. This case denied for all time the right of a state to control the action of the federal government. National supremacy, as stated in Article VI, is the most essential part of our system and *McCulloch* made it work. Had the case been decided the other way, our federal union would soon have been fragmented into small units, each of which could have taken unto itself the prerogatives of a nation.

Marshall continued to uphold and strengthen the

doctrine of national supremacy with *Cohens v. Virginia*[3] in 1821. The Cohens were arrested in Virginia for selling lottery tickets, legal under an Act of Congress within the District of Columbia. The decision meant that the Supreme Court had the power to pass on the constitutionality of state, as well as federal laws, and that the power of the states to legislate was subordinate to the provisions of the Constitution. Most of the Court's business from that day to this has involved cases challenging the validity of state laws and the fact that the court does have this power has meant that we have a diversity of state law but a unity of concept throughout all states, and that while states have freedom to enact laws dealing with local matters, all must conform to national guarantees.

From 1815-1860, this country saw an enormous expansion of trade and business. The use of corporations and trading companies, many of which did business in more than one state, produced numerous legal problems, often involving conflicts between the laws of different states. Respect for the Court increased as a growing feeling of nationalism began to replace sectional views, although concepts of sectionalism were to come to the fore again in the 1820's. With the growth of transportation, in particular, problems of multi-state business arose. Most states attempted to protect home-state industries by restricting the right of out-of-state merchants to do business. New York, in an effort to improve the steamboat business of its residents, passed laws providing that only New York steamboats could use its waterways. Steamboat companies from other states brought suit and the question reached the Supreme Court in 1824 as *Gibbons v. Ogden*.[4] Marshall held that Congress's power to regulate commerce "among the several states" meant that the federal government could regulate commerce within a state if it affected that of other states, hence the New York law permitting a monopoly was unconstitutional. It is directly on the doctrine of this case that the Supreme Court upheld Congress's power to legislate such things as the denial of the right of a restaurant owner to discriminate by race.

In order to have orderly expansion of business during this period, corporate stockholders needed assurance that the rights of corporations would be secure from state government's encroachments. The *Dartmouth College*[5] case in 1819 was Marshall's contribution to the growth of American corporation law. Dartmouth had been chartered by King George III in 1769. In 1816 the New Hampshire legislature, incited by Dartmouth's president, who did not care for the ideas of the Board of Trustees, attempted to alter its charter by adding more Board members who presumably would toe the legislature's line and, incidentally, transform the private college into a state university. Marshall's decision held that the charter could not be changed because it was a contract and Article I, Section 10 of the Constitution forbids states governments to "impair the obligation of a contract." As a result of this case, corporate expansion, so necessary to the growth of a predominantly rural nation, was protected from interference by those states in which legislators might prefer a more bucolic existence. When Marshall died in 1835, he had largely completed the job of insuring the stability of the federal union. Had someone of less ability been Chief Justice, the union might have failed.

The Taney Court and the Civil War — 1835-1866

Marshall's successor, Roger B. Taney, was appointed by President Jackson. By 1835 when Taney took his seat, Marshall had carved out the constitutional principles and his successor had only to consolidate the gains. Judicial supremacy was an unquestioned fact of American life. The industrial revolution was creating a dynamic economy and the new country was well on its way to stable life. However, after the *Dred Scott* decision in 1857, the Court's power and prestige were seriously impaired and the public acceptance of the Court, which marked the beginning of Taney's tenure in office, was severely eroded when he died in 1864.

Taney's first major decision was the 1837 *Charles River Bridge*[6] case. The Massachusetts legislature in 1785 granted authority to the Charles River Bridge Company for construction of a toll bridge across the Charles River from Boston. Tolls were to be collected indefinitely. In 1828 the legislature authorized construction of another bridge nearby and provided that tolls would be levied only to defray construction costs. Owners of the first bridge sought to enjoin construction of the second on the theory that the *Dartmouth* decision gave their company a complete monopoly, since a competing bridge would "impair the obligation of their contract." Taney ruled that the state had never surrendered its right to intervene in contracts on behalf of the public and that in this case the public interest required construction of another bridge. His opinion is still relevant today as we consider the right of an industry to produce in such a manner as to pollute the environment. He

wrote, "While the rights of private property are sacredly guarded, we must not forget that the community also have rights and that the happiness and well-being of every citizen depends on their faithful preservation." Taney was the first Justice to recognize the doctrine of the "public utility" — that a corporation providing a service vital to the public may be more strictly regulated than one which deals in a non-essential service. This decision aided competition in industrial areas and marked the beginning of a recognition of the state's police power, the right of the state to act to preserve the safety, health, good order and morals of its citizens. The change in attitude toward contracts which is shown by the contrast between this case and the *Dartmouth* case reflects the slow process by which the Court comes to change its mind on contracts or other matters in the light of economic or social change. This decision reflected the development of this country from a primarily rural society to one concerned with the problems inherent in the development of urban areas.

Our nation's greatest westward expansion occurred during this period. Westerners tended to be nationalistic and supremacy of the national government seemed assured. Slavery, however, had begun to be an important political problem, not only in the original states but in the new territories. The nadir of the Supreme Court's influence came when it tried to impose a legal solution to a political problem in the *Dred Scott* case. In 1820 the Missouri Compromise had admitted Maine as a free state and Missouri as slave, but all of the territories carved from the Louisiana Purchase north of Southern Missouri were declared to be free. The Compromise of 1850 admitted California as a free state, forbade slave trading in the District of Columbia and other territories were to be allowed to determine for themselves if they were slave or free. This Compromise quieted the fears of the slave states since it repealed the Missouri Compromise by implication and some of the states which chose to have slavery were north of the Southern boundary of Missouri. The Kansas-Nebraska Act of 1854 gave those two new territories the same choice and specifically repealed the Missouri Compromise.

Against that background the Supreme Court heard the *Dred Scott*[7] case in 1857. It involved a slave whose master had taken him to a free territory and had then returned him to a slave state. Scott sued to be declared free on the ground that he had gained irrevocable freedom as soon as he was on free soil. The case could have been settled by declaring that since Scott was a slave in the state in which he sued, he was not entitled to sue in the courts. The Court actually had precedent for refusing to hear the case at all. However, Chief Justice Taney, supported by a majority of his fellow justices, in a misguided effort to settle the question of slavery forever, succeeded in precipitating a judicial disaster. He delivered the majority opinion, which declared that since Scott was not a citizen in any state, he could not sue, and Taney concluded that the framers of the Constitution never intended blacks to be citizens at all. Secondly, the Court annulled Congress's efforts to legislate restrictions on slavery by declaring that since slaves were the property of their owners, freeing them deprived the owners of their property without due process of law. Reaction to this decision was immediate and severely damaged the Court's prestige. Anti-slavery people refused to recognize it and therefore the rule of law no longer served as a brake on emotionalism on either side of the argument. Congress could, of course, have amended the Constitution in substantially the same form as eventually enacted in the citizenship provisions of the 14th Amendment of 1868, but neither side was in a mood to be reasonable. President Buchanan made no effort to lead the people to calmness.

To Americans in 1861 it must have seemed that the Constitution was dead forever and none would have believed that the Court would ever have the prestige which it had enjoyed in Marshall's day. Between the election of Lincoln and his inauguration, seven states seceded. Buchanan announced that secession was unconstitutional but took no further action. The Civil War began on April 6, 1861.

Taney died in 1864 and was succeeded by Salmon P. Chase. Legal problems inevitably accompany war and never more than in a civil war. President Lincoln suspended the writ of habeas corpus and allowed searches and seizures without warrants and military arrests, all of which were at least constitutionally questionable, since Congress had never declared war, taking the position that since secession was illegal, no war existed against a hostile force. In 1861 in *ex parte Merryman*[8] the Court held that Lincoln's suspension of habeas corpus was unconstitutional, but he ignored the decision and, of course, then as now, the Court is powerless to enforce its orders without executive cooperation. Lincoln also put vast areas of the country under martial law and substituted courts-martial for civilian trials. In 1866 the Court heard the case of *ex parte Milligan*.[9] Milligan, a prominent Southern sympathizer, was tried and

sentenced to death by a military court in Indiana, which had been included under military jurisdiction although far removed from the battle area. The Court struck down the President's action, holding that military commissions could not act against civilians except in areas of open warfare where it was impossible for the civil courts to function. Since the Court's support originally had come from strong federalist areas, mainly the Northeast, which had been aghast at the *Scott* decision and were further infuriated by the Court's attempts to check the President, its prestige dropped to an all-time low.

After the Civil War, the Reconstruction Congress rode over the Constitution, the President and the Court. President Andrew Johnson was a special object of Congress's scorn because of his resistance to a policy of vengeance toward the South. Congress enacted legislation ending his right to supervise Reconstruction and set up a Joint Committee of the Congress. It passed a Civil Rights bill over his veto which was ratified as the 14th Amendment. Finally, in 1866 the radicals attempted to impeach him, and although he won by one vote, the prestige of the office was enormously degraded. The Court, in its turn, capitulated in attempts to reduce its power, thus reaching the low point of judicial independence in our history. However, as the more vehement firebrands aged and the White House changed hands, the Court and the President began to re-emerge as co-equal branches of the government.

Texas v. White,[10] 1869, was the end of the legal problems caused by secession. Texas had some federal bonds which the secessionist government sold to private investors to finance the war effort. When the investors tried to collect, the federal government refused to pay. The issue before the Court was whether or not Texas had the legal right to secede, since, if it had, it could legally have sold the bonds. The court held that the Union, once formed by vote of the people, was an indissoluble one and that no state had the legal right to withdraw. Therefore, regardless of the facts, the Southern states had never, as a matter of law, left the Union or ceased to be a part of the United States.

The *Legal Tender*[11] cases of 1871 reflect the growing differential between economic classes in the country. The federal government, in need of money to fight the war, had issued paper money instead of requiring gold as the medium of exchange. Inflation resulted, helping debtors and hurting creditors. When the Court held that the right to issue paper money was a constitutional one implied from the power to regulate currency, railroads and the budding corporations which had issued mortgages on their property to begin their businesses were delighted. Banks and other creditors were not.

After 1866, the economic realignment in this country affected the lives of many more citizens. As industry became more important, it created legal problems which had been unknown before the war. There is, for example, a great legal difference in the regulation of a village shoemaker who makes shoes in the back of his house and sells them in his parlor directly to the consumer and regulation of a giant shoe manufacturing corporation with factories in many states and sales outlets in all. The basic questions of whether the government had the right to regulate business and whether it ought to regulate business were to be the major interest of the Supreme Court for the next 70 years.

The Era of Big Business — 1866-1900

After the Civil War, America entered a period of economic expansion, resulting from the combination of abundant resources and the accessibility of railroads to move them. The war expenditures had helped Northern businessmen and, when it was over, they turned their energies to industrial expansion. Republicans were in the White House for most of the period and represented the business viewpoint. Railroads were the paramount industry because of their importance to expanding settlement of the plains areas and small railroads began to consolidate to cover more territory then each could alone. The oil, mail order and farm machine industries also thrived. The last twenty years of the 19th century were to become the pinnacle of success for big business. The legal climate was most condusive to enterprise. The courts of that time interpreted the 14th Amendment demand for "due process of law" in state action to include corporations as "citizens" and hence made them virtually immune to state regulation. Cases involving business occupied the Supreme Court continuously. The states had never had the power to regulate interstate railroads, although they frequently tried to do so, and the Interstate Commerce Act of 1887[12] attempted to do so. The income tax law of 1894 and the Sherman Antitrust Act of 1890[13] were all Congressional attempts to moderate the abuses of the new industrial giants, but the Court continued to favor business interests and eviscerated all of the Acts.

The 1872 *Slaughterhouse*[14] case was the first blow to federal regulation of business. The Louisiana legislature had given a monopoly on slaughtering animals in New Orleans to one company and hundreds of butchers found themselves without facilities. They asked the federal courts to interpret the "privileges and immunities" clause of the 14th Amendment to incorporate a new federally protected right to make a living, which in turn would declare the monopoly unconstitutional. However, the Supreme Court held that the clause did not add any rights, it merely protected pre-existing federal ones, such as the right of interstate travel, therefore the monopoly was a valid use of state power.

In 1876 in *Munn v. Illinois*,[15] the Supreme Court upheld a state's right of regulation. Chicago was the hub of the grain storage industry, since grain was stored there upon receipt from the Midwest's farmers until it could be distributed through the East. Munn and other warehousemen made agreements with railroads to get a monopoly on each line's incoming shipments and then fixed prices. This was most damaging to the grain merchants, who pressured the Illinois legislature into legislating against these practices in 1871. Warehouse owners claimed that these regulations deprived them of their property rights without due process of law. The Supreme Court decision was rendered by Chief Justice Morrison Waite, who had been appointed by President Grant upon Taney's death. He announced that although railroads were interstate commerce, grain storage was not and therefore the state regulations were valid. This was the last case in which the Supreme Court upheld any state regulation of business until 1937.

In addition to business cases, there were other problems as well. After Reconstruction officials left the South, the states began passing laws directed at the removal of the political rights the blacks had gained. For the first decade after the war, there were few "Jim Crow" laws requiring segregation, and integration was at least tolerated. However, persistent denials of the right to vote alarmed Congress and in 1875 the Civil Rights Act was enacted which protected the franchise and prohibited segregation in places of public accommodation. Several cases involving blacks who had been denied access to theatres and restaurants in New York City and other areas were decided by the Supreme Court in the *Civil Rights*[16] cases of 1883. The Court, delaying as long as possible, did not hear a case of this type during the 1870's. The Court held that the 14th Amendment, providing that "no state shall deny to any citizen the equal protection of the laws" applied only to state action and therefore, although official discrimination was prohibited, attempts to regulate private discrimination, as in restaurants, were unconstitutional. The results of this decision were the immediate segregation laws passed by every Southern state. Since political parties were not state organizations, the "white primary," in which the political party became a private club, was invented. A great deal of progress toward racial harmony had been achieved during the 1870's but the results of this decision and the one to follow in 1896, *Plessy v. Ferguson,* meant that by 1910 segregation laws were rigidly enforced throughout the South. The ironic aspect of this case is that an almost identical provision was enacted as part of the Civil Rights Act of 1964 and upheld by the Supreme Court, demonstrating again how the Court's attitudes change with changes in popular sentiment.

In 1886 the Supreme Court reached a clear turning point in commerce cases with *Wabash, St. Louis and Pacific Railway.*[17] It reversed the direction of the *Munn* case and held that state laws fixing maximum rates for transportation within the state where the rail line was part of an interstate system were unconstitutional because they violated the federal interstate commerce power. The concept of "laissez-faire" ("to leave alone") treatment of business was continued in 1890 in *Chicago, Milwaukee and St. Paul Railway v. Minnesota*[18] when the Court held that a legislature could not fix rates at all and that the question of "reasonableness" of rates was one which could be determined only by the judiciary.

At this time of minimal regulation of business, social problems caused by industrialization were becoming more acute. After the Civil War, increased industrialization induced many rural workers, both black and white, to migrate to urban areas to work in the mills. In addition to native workers, immigration was unrestricted and foreign workers poured in to swell the labor pool. All of these people converged on the low-rent areas of large cities and life in ghetto areas became deplorable. The erstwhile farm worker, once dependent on his initiative and the weather for his income, was totally dependent on his employer. There was no bargaining on wages or terms of employment. If he complained, he was fired. Employers bore no financial responsibility for industrial accidents and the worker, in addition to his pain, was often unemployable after his accident. Factories demanded long hours of work and child labor was the rule, since wages were so low the children had to help feed the family. The result of these conditions was the rise of the American labor movement and

social welfare legislation, but partially because of the attitude of the Supreme Court as well as the rest of the federal government, neither made progress until after 1935. In 1886 Samuel Gompers founded the American Federation of Labor, the first great union to survive until the present. In addition to refusing to recognize the right to strike, the Supreme Court during this period also struck down state attempts to enforce wage and hour laws.

A major event in the early labor movement was the arrest and conviction of Eugene V. Debs, an official of the American Railroad Union. The union was on strike in Chicago and a riot broke out when, although the Governor had not asked for his help, President Cleveland dispatched troops. Debs was arrested for violation of an injunction against the strike issued by a federal court in Chicago and the injunction which, in effect, killed the right to any strike, was upheld by the Supreme Court.[19] Only under the Clayton Act,[20] passed during President Wilson's term, was labor given the right to strike unimpeded by federal injunction.

As awareness of social problems caused by unregulated industry increased, Congress passed the Interstate Commerce Act of 1887, establishing the Interstate Commerce Commission, which eventually would be empowered to set rates in transportation. This was followed in 1890 by the Sherman Antitrust Act allowing Congress to regulate monopolies. In 1895, however, the Supreme Court destroyed the effect of the antitrust laws by its decision in the *E. C. Knight*[21] case. That sugar refining company was about to merge with others which would have controlled over a third of the sugar production in the country. Alleging that this was a conspiracy in restraint of trade, the government asked for a court order to stop it. The Supreme Court held that although Congress could regulate transportation and shipment of the sugar after refining, manufacturing was not in interstate commerce and any attempt to regulate it was unconstitutional. Since companies involved in the big trusts always had plants in more than one state, the net effect was that manufacturing monopolies were not regulated by either state or federal governments.

Also in 1895, the Court struck down the graduated income tax which had been enacted by Congress in 1894. The Court held in *Pollock v. Farmer's Loan and Trust Company*[22] that a graduated income tax (one in which the tax rate goes up as the taxable income rises) was an unconstitutional violation of the provision in Article I that direct taxes had to be uniform throughout the states. This decision was overcome by the 16th Amendment, but it was not ratified until 1913. This case struck at the Marshall doctrine in *McCulloch* that the federal government could intervene in state business whenever the ends were national. At this point, with very little restriction on business and very insignificant taxes, big business was in its heyday. It is at this period that J. P. Morgan, the financier, was supposed to have said "the public be damned," an attitude which was not uncommon in his social circle.

The Court reached the end of the 19th century with the case of *Plessy v. Ferguson*.[23] After the *Civil Rights* case, most Southern states had enacted segregation laws requiring blacks to sit in separate cars on trains traveling intrastate. Since all states in the South had them, it was, in effect, an interstate ban. Plessy, a New Orleans black, was arrested for sitting in a "white" car on a train. When he challenged the law before the Supreme Court, it held that the 14th Amendment only forbade *unequal* protection of the laws and as long as facilities were equivalent, separate-but-equal statutes were constitutional. As a result of this case, those states which had neglected to pass segregation laws after the *Civil Rights* cases hastened to do so, and by 1910, "Jim Crow" reigned throughout the South. Separate-but-equal remained the law of the land until 1954 when the Supreme Court held that "separate" was inherently "unequal."

As the century closed, the Court virtually killed the Interstate Commerce Commission's powers in the 1897 case of *Cincinnati, New Orleans and Texas Railway v. I.C.C.*[24] by denying the Commission the power to set rates. The decision of the sixteen cases from 1897 to 1906 involving the Commission before the Supreme Court resulted in only one victory for the Commission and at the turn of the century it was completely powerless.

1900-1937

Theodore Roosevelt became President in 1901 and spearheaded a revival of the concept of nationalism. Within the next decade a reform movement against business abuses began bringing about a new concept of federal police power in prosecution of monopolies and the revitalization of the Interstate Commerce Commission.

The first case allowing use of the interstate commerce clause to regulate public health, morals or safety was *Champion v. Ames*[25] of 1903. The Supreme Court upheld federal laws prohibiting interstate transportation of lottery tickets, a statute motivated by Congress's attempts to halt gambling. The following year the Court upheld, in *McCray v. U.S.*,[26] a federal excise tax on colored margarine passed by Congress after lobbying by the dairy industry. This decision opened a vast area for federal social control by taxation, but subsequent cases again narrowed its impact until the 1930's.

Congress enacted a great deal of legislation to control the increasing tendency of business toward monopoly and substandard production. The Interstate Commerce Commission was strengthened by the Elkins Act of 1903[27] and the Hepburn Act of 1906[28] which gave the Commission the power to fix all transportation rates. The Pure Food and Drug Act[29] and the Meat Inspection Act[30] were both passed in 1906, largely as a result of public nausea after reading Upton Sinclair's *The Jungle,* depicting conditions in meat processing plants.

However, in spite of *Champion v. Ames* and the *McCray* case, the Supreme Court, unlike the other two branches of government, held firmly to a policy of non-interference with business and most attempts to regulate it were declared unconstitutional. In 1905 the Court, in *Lochner v. New York*[31] found a state statute limiting the maximum hours a baker could work to 10 a day or 60 a week to be an "unreasonable" use of the state's police power which interfered with the baker's freedom of contract. In 1908, however, the Court accepted the new-fangled notion of state regulation of wages and hours for women in *Muller v. Oregon*.[32] The case involved a state law restricting hours for women workers and the Court upheld it as a reasonable use of the state police power. In addition to the landmark holding, the case was also famous because it was the first one in which a "Brandeis brief" was used. Louis D. Brandeis, to be appointed to the Court by President Wilson in 1916, was the attorney for Oregon. Instead of restricting his argument to law, he demonstrated by medical and sociological evidence what effect long hours of work had on women. Unlike the *Lochner* case, in which the Court concluded that "everybody knew" it did not hurt bakers to work, Brandeis convinced them that there was a social danger if the law were overturned. This was the first case in many years to break the barrier of the Court's economic theory of laissez-faire, and although there would be a return to conservatism, the Brandeis view would eventually prevail.

Since the 1895 *E. C. Knight* case, the government had been so sure that the Court would knock down attempts to enforce the antitrust laws that it did not bring any suits. However, in 1904 the Court upheld the government's contention that the *Northern Securities Railroad*[33] trust was a conspiracy in restraint of trade. In 1905 the government again won against the *Swift & Co.*[34] meatpacking combine. The Court broadened its view of "interstate commerce", holding that although all the packing houses were in Chicago, they "affected the stream of interstate commerce" and therefore could be regulated. The Court distinguished it from the *Knight* case by declaring that Swift was engaged in sales, not production. The Court's inclination to permit regulation of business continued as it recognized the authority of the Interstate Commerce Commission in *ICC v. Illinois Central Railroad*[35] in 1910 and in 1914 *U.S. v. Atchison, Topeka & Santa Fe.*[36] Finally realizing that the social and economic problems occasioned by big business required a new look at the Constitution, the Court paved the way for President Wilson to ask Congress for legislation establishing other regulatory commissions, including the Federal Trade Commission, the Tariff Commission and the Federal Reserve Board.

In 1911, however, the Court returned to its views of laissez-faire economics. In *Standard Oil v. U.S.*,[37] the Court held that the Sherman Antitrust Act did not automatically prohibit all monpoly, it just permitted restraint of "unreasonable" monopolies and the Court did not find that Standard Oil was "unreasonable". This again made it almost impossible to break a monopoly, since all of them could argue that they were "reasonable". However, the Court at the same time was willing to accept government regulation for which it could apply the concept of "reasonableness". In the *Hipolite Egg Co.*[38] case of 1911, the Court agreed that the Pure Food and Drug Administration had the authority to seize contaminated food.

President Wilson's term began in 1913 with a desire for more control over big business. During his tenure in office, the Clayton Antitrust Act[39] was passed in 1915 forbidding price discrimination and other conspiracies. It also was the first federal law which granted any power to labor and denied the federal courts the right of injunction to stop a nonviolent strike, thus reversing the Supreme Court's 1895 *Debs* decision. The Adamson Act[40] of 1916 provided an eight-hour day for railway workers, again under the interstate commerce clause, and the Court upheld it in 1917 in *Wilson v. New.*[41] However, in 1918 the Court minimized the effect of the *Muller* case by outlawing, in *Hammer v. Dagenhart*,[42] a child labor law which Congress had passed in 1916.

Since the *Knight* ruling prohibited regulation of manufacturing, Congress attempted to restrict shipment of good which had been made by children. The theory behind the Act was that goods which were not shipped could not be sold, hence child labor would become unprofitable. However, the Court invalidated the Act, although they admitted the right of the government to seize goods in the *Hipolite Egg* case. The difference, according to the Court, was that the contaminated eggs were harmful in themselves but that the goods made by the children were not, thus the indirect attempt to regulate manufacturing impinged upon the reserve powers of the states under the 10th Amendment. This case was not reversed until 1941 in *U.S. v. Darby.*

For the first time since the Civil War, major civil liberties cases came to the Court during and after World War I. Oliver Wendell Holmes, Jr. had been appointed to the Court in 1902 by President Roosevelt and he won his name as "The Great Dissenter" in cases involving freedom of expression in wartime. Holmes, whose opinions are widely considered the most literary in the Court's history, frequently disagreed with his fellow justices, but time and changing attitudes have seen his opinions become the law of the land within several decades. During World War I, there was considerable hysteria in the country about anything suspected of being "unpatriotic". Violent reactions against anything German meant that study of the German language was made illegal in numerous states and German operas were never sung. Any difference of opinion was labeled "sedition" and Wilson, as Lincoln had done, attempted to impose conformity by legislation. The Espionage Act of 1917 banned anything the Postmaster General, using any standard he chose, thought was "seditious" from the mail, and at one point both the *New York Times* and the *Saturday Evening Post* were included. With Holmes writing the opinion, the Espionage Act was found unconstitutional as a violation of the right of free speech in *Schenck v. U.S.*[43] in 1919. It was this opinion which established the "clear and present danger" rule — that basic freedoms in this country cannot be restricted unless the government can prove an obvious and immediate danger. However, since the War was over before the Court's decision was rendered, it was of little practical effect.

The theory of nationalism was still predominant in federal-state relations. In 1920 the Court upheld a treaty made with Canada dealing with migratory birds. A previous law prohibiting hunting of certain species of birds had been declared unconstitutional on the grounds that there was no implied power on this subject (birds, since they did not belong to anyone, were not in interstate commerce). However, when the same provisions were included in a treaty, the Court held that the inherent powers of government to conduct foreign relations mean that a treaty is valid as long as it does not include something which is specifically prohibited by the Constitution. This decision, *Missouri v. Holland*,[44] strengthened the power of the President to make treaties as he saw fit.

During the 1920's the Court again retreated to its laissez-faire view of business. The result of the Court's decisions since the 1880's meant that widespread fraud in stock manipulations could not be regulated, although Congress made no effort to do so in any case, and there was almost no control over credit. Instead of a solid economy, the American business scene was much more like a balloon, as the Crash of 1929 demonstrated, but the Court remained aloof from the realities of the situation and refused to allow any more regulation of business until the *Nebbia* case of 1934.

In 1923 in *Adkins v. Children's Hospital*[45] the Court ignored its decision in the *Muller* case and invalidated a law which restricted hours of work for female employees in the District of Columbia. Again, as in the *Lochner* case, the Court held that this was a denial of the right of women to work and interference with their "liberty of contract". The language of this decision is the classic exposition of the traditional doctrine of laissez-faire economics. This case was eventually overruled in 1937 in *West Coast Hotel Co. v. Parrish,* but laws prohibiting overtime for female employees are now challenged by women themselves, who no longer want extra protection.

The Court's respect for individualism went beyond contracts and into the field of civil liberties. In 1883 the Court had held in *Hurtado v. California*[46] that the 14th Amendment did not require states to abide by the procedural restraints in the 4th, 5th, 6th and 8th Amendments which applied to federal criminal prosecutions, and the period of the 20's was the first sign that this view would be altered. As a reaction to anti-German feeling during World War I, states had passed laws forbidding the teaching of foreign languages to children in public schools. *Myer v. Nebraska*[47] in 1923 declared these to be unconstitutional restrictions on the right of a parent to bring up his children according to his individual conscience. In 1925 this was followed by *Pierce v. Society of Sisters,*[48] which invalidated laws forbidding parents to send their children to private schools. The main themes of these cases, that a parent has a right to educate his child, were picked up in the "School Prayer" cases several decades later. These two cases were decided under the 14th Amendment alone. However, the first case in which a specific right in the Bill of Rights was declared applicable to the states was *Gitlow v. New York*[49] in 1925. This case, involving freedom of speech, was a landmark decision of the court and paved the way for most of the civil liberties cases of the past thirty years. The Court overruled the *Hurtado* decision and declared that when a state denied free speech it denied to its people "due process of law" as required by the 14th Amendment. This concept of "incorporation" of the Bill of Rights by the 14th Amendment is now almost complete. *Gitlow* was expanded in 1938 by *Near v. Minnesota*[50] and *Powell v. Alabama*[51] which incorporated the basic rights of criminal procedure, declaring that defendants who are denied counsel are denied a federally protected right. The concept of incorporation of provisions of the Bill of Rights as restrictions on state police power was almost uniformly accepted by 1932, although not until the 1960's were all major rights incorporated.

The President's powers also grew in the 20's. The *Missouri* case had strengthened his hand in treaty-making and *Myers v. U.S.*[52] in 1926 increased his power in dealing with the government. Myers, a postmaster, had been appointed by the President and confirmed by the Senate but before his term was up, the President fired him. He sued for his lost salary and the Supreme Court upheld the President's right to dismiss an employee of the executive branch. A 1935 case was to restrict this right as to employees of independent commissions, but the President had vast new control over the bureaucracy.

In 1929 the glorious dream of economic abundance burst and the Great Depression was at hand. President Hoover, although lamenting the problems, took an extremely limited view of his constitutional authority to act and so intervened in only limited ways as banks, business and necessary production collapsed. Things did not improve, and President Franklin Roosevelt's victory was a vote for immediate federal intervention in the crisis. Roosevelt sent numerous proposals to Congress designed to stop the collapse of the economy and used his executive authority to close the banks and to stop mortgage foreclosures. The "New Deal" concepts as his proposals were termed, were enacted at an extremely rapid rate by Congress, which was beyond the point of reflection on the possible unconstitutionality of the measures as long as they would work.

In 1934 the Supreme Court upheld, in *Nebbia v. New York*,[53] a state statute creating a board to fix milk prices. This marked the reversal of the decisions of the 20's in which the Court had struck down most statutes of this type. The *Nebbia* case allowed a state, within its police power, to make any regulations it deemed necessary for the public welfare, again demonstrating that the Court's view of new situations requires it to adopt new interpretations.

The regulatory agencies gained tremendous independence as a result of *Humphrey's Executor v. U.S.*[54] Humphrey had been appointed to the Federal Trade Commission by President Hoover, but before his term expired, President Roosevelt fired him. The Court, denying this power to the executive, distinguished this from the *Myers* case by holding that Myers was an employee of the executive department but that regulatory commissioners were not, since they were answerable only to the judicial and legislative branches of government and that, in fact, the commissions had been established to be as remote from presidential political influence as possible. The *Humphrey* case did for the commissions as much as the attempt to impeach Justice Chase in 1805 had done to sustain the principle of judicial independence.

The Court construed many New Deal laws as an unconstitutional delegation of legislative power to the executive. In January 1935, the Court issued ten decisions on New Deal legislation and struck down eight laws. In particular, the *Panama Refining Company*[55] case throttled the President's plan to regulate the oil industry. The Court held that when Congress passed a law giving the executive the right to regulate an industry without fixing standards, it had unconstitutionally delegated its lawmaking powers. The Court also struck down the National Industrial Recovery Act of 1933 in the *Schechter Poultry Co.*[56] case. The NIRA had used codes of wages, prices and marketing procedures which the President had allowed the affected industries to compose and again the Court said that these regulations were an unconstitutional delegation of Congress's power. The Agricultural Adjustment Act and the Bituminous Coal Act, both of which also regulated marketing procedures, were declared unconstitutional for the same reason. In *Carter v. Carter Coal Co.*,[57] the Court also said that regulation of coal production was per se invalid under the doctrine of the Knight case.

The basic issue in the country as the result of these decisions was the Court's refusal, at a crucial time in American life, to accept the concept of constitutional growth. Roosevelt and many of those of his political persuasion were furious with the Court, and the President's method of retaliation was known as the "Court-packing plan". Roosevelt interpreted his re-election in 1936 as a mandate from the people to continue his policies. In hopes of strengthening his position with the Court, he proposed to Congress that a new federal judge be named for each remaining on the Court after reaching age 70, which would have increased the membership of the Supreme Court to fifteen.

Tampering with the structure of the judicial branch was too much for Congress, even though a majority of its members disagreed with the Court, so the plan went down to defeat. However, the Court realized in the face of this threat that unless they bowed to the wishes of the people, the effectiveness of the judicial branch would be lost forever. Thus occurred "the switch in time which saved nine". In March, 1937, the Court reversed the *Adkins* case of 1923 and upheld minimum wages and maximum hours for women in *West Coast Hotel Co. v. Parrish*.[58] In *National Labor Relations Board v. Jones & Laughlin Steel Co.*[59] they upheld the right of the National Labor Relations Board to regulate all aspects of commerce, including production of goods which would be shipped in interstate commerce, thus finally overruling the doctrine of the *Knight* case. The Court also upheld the Social Security Act,[60] reversing its old idea that taxation could not be used to promote social welfare. These cases marked a definite break with the restrictive interpretation of "interstate commerce" which the Court had espoused for many years.

The year 1937 marked the end of a period of American history in which one group, business, dominated the economic scene, and by the end of that year, a more balanced social structure, with regard for the farmer and the worker, had replaced one-group rule. This was the end of the concept of the application of "due process" in economic matters and from that time until the present, "due process" has been used exclusively in cases involving individual liberties under the Bill of Rights. A new era of federal regulatory power was at hand. The New Deal changed the public's concept of the role the federal government should play in the economic sphere and "dual federalism", which left large areas of regulation to the states, was almost entirely dead. These constitutional changes were wide in their ramifications and today the federal government exercises wide control over our lives, but all these changes have taken place within the established structures of our government, and again, a flexible Constitution had met and overcome national problems.

1938-1953

Continuing its new economic policy, in 1938 the Court upheld federal enforcement of the rights of labor in a series of cases involving the National Labor Relations Board. The Court held that if interstate commerce were even remotely affected, the national government could regulate production. In the 1938 case of *U.S. v. Carolene Products Co.*,[61] the Court said "regulatory legislation affecting ordinary commercial transactions is not to be pronounced unconstitutional unless it is of such a character as to preclude the assumption that it rests upon some rational basis within the knowledge of the legislature." Since it is almost impossible to show that a legislature is irrational, few, if any, attempts have been successful. In 1941 the Court upheld the child labor provisions of the Fair Labor Standard Act[62] in *U.S. v. Darby*,[63] thus overruling *Hammer v. Dagenhart*. *Mulford v. Smith*,[64] 1939, established the constitutionality of federal agriculture regulation and the Court also permitted federal regulation of public utilities. In 1940, in *Madden v. Kentucky*[65] the Court finally said that the concept that a corporation was a "citizen" for purposes of 14th Amendment protection was overruled and the era of the Court's efforts to block industrial regulation was over.

With the end of its preoccupation with economics cases, the Court entered a period of attention to individual liberties under the Bill of Rights. Since the beginning of this period, the Court has tried to establish a system of justice which will eventually realize the promises of liberty for which our Revolution had been fought.

The Civil Liberties Era began with *Palko v. Connecticut*[66] in 1937. This case, involving the constitutionality of state laws affecting freedom of speech, incorporated for all time those provisions in the Bill of Rights "essential to the concept of ordered liberty" into the 14th Amendment. *DeJonge v. Oregon*[67] held that the right to participate in orderly political meetings was a federally protected right under the 1st Amendment and unless there was open advocacy of violence, the state could not restrict it. *Herndon v. Lowry*,[68] the third free-speech case that year, re-established Justice Holmes's "clear and present danger" rule which had been ignored for many years. The 1937 case of *Senn v. Tile Layers Union*[69] added to the list of "incorporated rights" the right of peaceful picketing and *Hague v. C.I.O.*[70]

added the right of peaceable assembly. *Cantwell v. Connecticut*[71] added freedom of religion to the list of rights with which the state could not interfere, and *Thornhill v. Alabama*[72] and *Lovell v. Griffin*,[73] both of 1938, added the right to distribute pamphlets and to organize politically. These concepts were carried over in the 1943 "Flag Salute"[74] cases in which the Court held that children who have religious objections to saluting the flag at school cannot, by any stretch of the imagination, be held to present a "clear and present danger" to the community. *Bridges v. California*[75] extended 1st Amendment protection to newspapers, declaring unconstitutional California laws which provided criminal penalties for newspapers which criticized the government. In 1946 the Court declared[76] that an attempt by Congress to cut the salaries of three government employees whom the House Un-American Activities Committee had declared "subversive" was an attempt to use the constitutionally forbidden device of a bill of attainder. All these cases throughout the 1940's and early 50's rested on a very broad interpretation of 1st Amendment freedoms.

In addition to the 1st Amendment cases, the late 30's and early 40's saw the genesis of a trend of civil rights cases which culminated in 1954 in *Brown v. Board of Education*,[77] which held that racial discrimination was unconstitutional. In 1938, although the Court did not specifically overrule "separate but equal," it held in *Missouri ex rel. Gaines v. Canada*[78] that facilities had to be equal in fact. Missouri had no law school for blacks and refused to admit them to the white law school, so the Court held that it must either build a new one for blacks immediately or admit them to the one it had. This decision marked the beginning of a new judicial mood toward blacks and was followed by *Sweatt v. Painter*[79] in 1950, which held that the black law school in Texas was inherently unequal because unless all law students have the same opportunities to meet those with whom they would later practice, they did not have an equal chance for education. *McLaurin v. Oklahoma*[80] in the same year held that students, once admitted, must be treated equally and may not be segregated in classes, the library or the cafeteria.

Under the concept of "state action" in the 1875 *Civil Rights* cases, the Southern political parties had declared themselves to be private clubs and restricted the right to vote in the primaries to whites. *Smith v. Allwright*[81] in 1944 held that since the primary was an integral part of the electoral process, it had to be open to all. In addition to political rights, the Court also made new restrictions on "separate-but-equal." In 1941, *Mitchell v. U.S.*[82] held that denial of Pullman berths on trains to Negroes when they were provided for whites was a denial of equal protection of the laws, and in 1950 *Henderson v. U.S.*[83] forbade discrimination in railroad dining cars, since railroads were within the power of the federal government to regulate.

In the field of property rights, the 1948 case of *Shelley v. Kraemer*[84] forbade the judicial enforcement by civil suits of restrictive covenants in deeds. The Court could not outlaw provisions in deeds requiring purchasers to agree to resell only to whites, but it did declare that when law suits were brought to enforce them, state action was involved and hence the 14th Amendment was violated. The stage was thus set for the far-reaching decision of the Warren Court in the middle 50's and beyond which effectively rendered all segregation unconstitutional.

World War II again saw the country in crisis. President Roosevelt adopted the theory that war gave the executive sweeping emergency powers and the Supreme Court usually backed him up. As far back as 1936 in *U.S. v. Curtiss-Wright*,[85] the Court had held that the president's inherent powers in the field of foreign relations gave him the power to provide criminal penalties for shipping arms to foreign nations. This concept of "inherent executive power" was adhered to by the Court throughout the war. Roosevelt, as Commander-in-Chief, dispatched destroyers to our European Allies before we actually entered the war. After Pearl Harbor, by executive order derived from broad grants of authority from Congress, he created innumerable boards to regulate rationing, price control, production, labor disputes and hundreds of other areas of life. In 1944 the Court sustained them in *Yakus v. U.S.*[86]

The civil liberties of 112,000 Japanese-Americans were completely ignored by an executive order which permitted the Army to remove them from their homes on the West Coast and intern them in detention camps for periods of up to four years, solely on the grounds that they were of Japanese descent. There was no attempt to distinguish between the loyal and the disloyal and they were just herded away. The 1944 case of *Korematsu v. U.S.*[87] upheld the detention on the theory that in a time of national emergency, the Army and the president have powers which they do not ordinarily possess, and that the suspension of the right to habeas corpus was therefore valid. Such orders would not be declared constitutional today, but during the fever which affected the Court as well as the country in wartime, constitutional "niceties" were sometimes overlooked. *Ex parte Quirin*[88] of 1942 held that a German spy in this country could be court-martialed instead of being tried in federal court and *In re Yamashita*[89] held that a Japanese General on trial for war crimes had no constitutional rights at all. The 1945 cases of *Cramer v. U.S*[90] had held that before any American citizen could be tried for treason, it had to be shown that he actively helped the enemy's agents instead of just hiding them, but in 1947 *Haupt v. U.S.*[91] held that merely housing a spy was enough.

Although in retrospect what was done to the Japanese-Americans who were not guilty of anything except not being white sounds as if the country was not interested in any constitutional rights, with that most unbelievable exception (since the war was being fought to oppose race hatred), the Constitution did survive the war and its flexibility was demonstrated.

After the war this country embarked on a period of unparalleled involvement with the rest of the world. The period saw our involvement in the birth of the United Nations, a far cry from the isolationism abroad in the land when the Senate refused to ratify the League of Nations treaty. The beginnings of the "Cold War" brought numerous defense treaties, such as our NATO involvement, in which we pledged our aid to our allies if attacked.

The Korean War was not a declared war, but President Truman dispatched troops to fight under his authority as Commander-in-Chief, asking afterwards for a Congressional Resolution of support, which he got after heated debate. The president's power in time of a "police action" was, however, not to equal the emergency powers held by a president in a declared war. During World War II President Roosevelt had seized several companies during time of labor difficulties in an effort to keep war materials production going. President Truman attempted to do the same thing to the steel mills when the Steelworkers' Union went out on strike during the Korean Conflict. However in 1952 in *Youngstown Sheet & Tube Co. v. Sawyer*[92] the Court found no statutory authority for his action and thus the seizure was unconstitutional. This was the first substantial check on presidential power since the New Deal days.

During the early '50's, the country embarked on a rather hysterical subversive witch-hunt spearheaded by Senator Joseph McCarthy, who was eventually censured by the Senate for his actions. The Congress passed numerous laws dealing with subversive activity and put new teeth into the Smith Act[93] of 1940 which had regulated speech which might be construed as an attempt to overthrow the government. Between 1948 and 1954, the Supreme Court upheld most of the laws as constitutional, although subsequently the Warren Court watered them down. In *American Communications Ass'n v. Douds*[94] in 1950 the Court upheld the constitutionality of a requirement in the Taft-Hartley Act which required unions to sign non-communist affidavits, on the theory that this was a valid use of the interstate commerce power. In *Dennis v. U.S.*,[95] 1951, the Court upheld the Smith Act provision requiring registration of those belonging to organizations which the Attorney-General thought subversive. This case was extremely significant, since the previous law, to which the Warren Court was to return, had been that before one could be prosecuted for belonging to an organization, it had to be proven that not only did one belong, he had joined knowing that the organization sought to overthrow the government and had actively participated personally in illegal activities. The Smith Act declared that mere membership was enough to prove subversion, but *Wieman v. Updegraff*[96] in 1952 partially returned to the "knowledge" rule.

Other than in the field of sedition, the post-war Court rapidly increased the number of provisions in the Bill of Rights which it protected from state intervention by incorporation into the 14th Amendment. The 1949 decision in *Terminiello v. Chicago*[97] declared that a speaker whose remarks result in a riot is not liable for prosecution if the riot is caused by those who disagree with him as long as he himself is peaceable. In *Roth v. U.S.*[98] the Court sharply curtailed the right of censorship of allegedly "obscene" material and in *Burstyn v. Wilson*,[99] 1952, the Court held that movies may not be censured on the grounds that they are "sacreligious." In the field of freedom of religion, the Court enunciated many new cases upholding the doctrine of separation of church and state, and upheld the idea that the individual has the right to his own religious belief even if it is abhorrent to the rest of the community. *Everson v. Board of Education*,[100] 1947, in dealing with a state law providing free school bus transportation to children attending parochial schools, upheld the practice as an aid to the children, not to religion. However in 1948 in *McCollum v. Board of Education*,[101] the Court declared that a state could not impose religious ideas on children by using public school facilities for teaching religion, although in 1952 it upheld "released time" whereby children could be excused from

school to go to a church for religious instruction.

Thus at the mid-point of the 1950's, while the Court was not willing to adopt the position that a possible political subversive had 1st Amendment rights which could overcome the danger he presented to the community, the 1st Amendment in other contexts was brought more firmly under the "preferred position" doctrine, in which, before a state or the federal government could infringe on 1st Amendment rights, it had to demonstrate a more overwhelming necessity than it was required to use in other areas.

1953-1969
The "Warren Court" began in 1953 when President Eisenhower appointed Earl Warren as Chief Justice, a position which he held until his retirement in 1969. In general terms, the Warren Court gave an emphasis new in American history to the personal rights of citizens. In the areas of civil rights, 1st Amendment freedoms, restrictions on the states' use of criminal procedures to deny fair trials and political rights, the Warren Court focused on the individual in society.

1969-1986
Chief Justice Warren E. Burger took office on June 24, 1969, and the "Warren Court" era was over. He resigned in 1986 to chair the nation's celebration of the Bicentennial of the Constitution. While numerous people felt that the newly constituted court would be substantially more conservative, that was not the case. While the court proceeded more slowly in finding new directions for some aspects of the law, few of the landmark decisions from the Warren era were overruled. A "conservative" justice, for example, wrote the decision which revolutionized the abortion laws in this country. Especially in the field of racial discrimination, the Burger court was as active as the Warren court.

In 1981, Justice Sandra Day O'Connor, who had not been able to get a job with a law firm at the time she graduated with honors from Stanford Law School (because almost no law firms hired women in the 1950's) became the first woman member of the Supreme Court of the United States. In the early 1970's, the number of women in law schools and entering the practice of law had begun to increase remarkably. It is still too soon for many of this group of young women to achieve positions of power within the profession, but it will be interesting to find out if this development will cause any major changes in the American legal system.

In 1986 President Ronald Reagan named Justice William H. Rehnquist as Chief Justice to succeed Chief Justice Burger. Justice Rehnquist had been appointed to the Supreme Court by President Nixon and took his seat on the Court on January 7, 1982.

No one knows what new directions the Supreme Court will take in the future. Presumably John Marshall never thought when he read his opinion in *McCulloch v. Maryland* to the waiting country that its effects would put the federal government into a position of regulation such as it occupies today. We do know, however, that our Constitution will stand above the pressures of political expediency and as its interpretations change in the future as they have in the past, we can be confident that it will continue to be, as it has been through our history, the bedrock on which we will build "liberty and justice for all."

The Preamble

WE THE PEOPLE of the United States, in Order to form a more perfect Union, establish Justice, insure domestic Tranquility, provide for the common defence, promote the general Welfare, and secure the Blessings of Liberty to ourselves and our Posterity, do ordain and establish this CONSTITUTION for the United States of America.

THE AUTHORITY of our Constitution was given by the consent of the people of all the states and was not the act of the independent state governments. Although delegates to the Constitutional Convention had been elected by the state legislatures, the Constitution was submitted to the people for ratification, not to the legislatures. Our government, therefore, proceeds directly from the people and was established by them. In 1819 the Supreme Court upheld this view of the source of the Constitution's authority in *McCulloch v. Maryland*,[1] probably the most famous judicial decision in our history.

Whether the Constitution was established by the people or by an agreement among the states is not an unimportant question. Throughout our history some people have felt that the United States government and its Constitution came into being by action of the state governments. This is known as the "states' rights" or "compact" view of constitutional interpretation. Implied in the theory that all the national government's powers come from grants by the states is an idea known as "interposition." Those who believe in interposition believe that the United States is nothing more than a group of fifty states and that any state may impose its power within its borders against any decision of the Supreme Court or any act of Congress. In effect, this doctrine holds that a state does not have to respect those decisions of the United States Supreme Court with which it does not agree. This is, as you can see, a theory very similar to that which existed at the time of the Articles of Confederation. The keystone of this thesis was disavowed in the Preamble of our Constitution and by Article VI.[2]

Although the Preamble indicates by whom the Constitution was established and the general purposes for which the people ordained it, it has never been regarded as the source of any specific powers conferred on any branch of the government.[3] Such powers arise only from specific grants in the body of the Constitution or those which may be implied from those specific grants.

The purpose of the Preamble is to expound the nature, extent and application of the powers actually conferred by the Constitution and not to create them.

The Preamble is a clear indication that the founders were not just a group of men creating a government which would serve their own narrow, selfish interests, but that they were statesmen dedicated to establishing a government which would serve the common good for many generations. Two hundred years of success prove the wisdom of their political theories.

Article One

Article I of the Constitution deals with the Congress, the legislative branch of the federal government. The Congress, rather than the President, is vested by the Constitution with the lawmaking function and the President is restricted to recommending laws thought wise, vetoing of laws considered bad and seeing to the faithful execution of laws properly enacted by Congress.[1] This article describes the composition of the two Houses of Congress (the Senate and the House of Representatives), the requirements for election to either House and the powers and duties of this branch of the government. It also specifically forbids Congress and the states to do certain specified things.

The framers of the Constitution envisioned the Congress as the most important and most powerful branch of the government. Our constitutional practice grows by custom and usage as well as by amendment, and the growth of the legislative power of the President is one way in which it has been quite startling. Today much of the important legislation is initiated by the President and members of his executive departments. When you read in the newspaper that "The President sent a bill to Congress today," you should remember that George Washington never sent bills to Congress. Historically speaking, this is a recent use of Presidential power.

One of the major political questions at the present time is the proper division of power between the President and the Congress, particularly in matters relating to the conduct of military affairs. Representatives and Senators on committees such as Foreign Affairs and Armed Services are often in conflict with the President's representatives, such as the Secretaries of Defense and State, about whose business it is to send troops and carry on military operations.

The Gramm-Rudman Hollings Act, designed to reduce the federal financial deficit which by 1986 had begun to cause the nation serious economic problems, required reductions in federal spending. If Congress and the President did not agree on spending cuts, they would be made automatically by the Comptroller-General of the United States based on percentages specified in the legislation. The Supreme Court held the Act unconstitutionally in violation of the doctrine of separation of powers, since it vested executive authority, which belongs to the President, in the hands of the Comptroller-General, who is subservient to Congress.[2]

SECTION 1

All legislative Powers herein granted shall be vested in a Congress of the United States, which shall consist of a Senate and House of Representatives.

There are two Houses of Congress. The Senate has two members from each state and the House of Representatives consists of members apportioned on the basis of population. Every ten years the federal government takes a census to determine how many people live in each state, and a state may gain or lose representatives on the basis of this survey.

This bicameral system was fixed at the Constitutional Convention as a result of the "Connecticut Compromise." The big states, quite naturally, wanted a Congress whose membership would be determined by population. The smaller states wanted a legislature in which each state would have the same number of representatives. When the Convention was about to collapse as a result of disagreement on this very fundamental issue, the Connecticut Compromise saved the day, the Convention and our system of government.

SECTION 2

1 The House of Representatives shall be composed of Members chosen every second Year by the People of the several States, and the Electors in each State shall have the Qualifications requisite for Electors of the most numerous Branch of the State Legislature.

2 No Person shall be a Representative who shall not have attained to the Age of twenty-five Years, and been seven Years a Citizen of the United States, and who shall not, when elected, be an Inhabitant of that State in which he shall be chosen.

3 [Representatives and direct Taxes shall be apportioned among the several States which may be included within this Union, according to their respective Numbers, which shall be determined by adding to the whole Number of free Persons, including those bound to Service for a Term of Years, and excluding Indians not taxed, three fifths of all other Persons.] The actual Enumeration shall be made within three Years after the first Meeting of the Congress of the United States, and within every subsequent Term of ten Years, in such Manner as they shall by Law direct. The Number of Representatives shall not exceed one for every thirty Thousand, but each State shall have at Least one Representative; and until such enumeration shall be made, the State of New Hampshire shall be entitled to chuse three, Massachusetts eight, Rhode-Island and Providence Plantations one, Connecticut five, New-York six, New Jersey four, Pennsylvania eight, Delaware one, Maryland six, Virginia ten, North Carolina five, South Carolina five, and Georgia three.

4 When vacancies happen in the Representation from any State, the Executive Authority thereof shall issue Writs of Election to fill such Vacancies.

5 The House of Representatives shall chuse their Speaker and other Officers; and shall have the sole Power of Impeachment.

CLAUSE 1 Elections are held every two years for all 435 members of the House of Representatives. The men who wrote the Constitution felt that a short term of office would force the Representatives to remain in close touch with the people whom they represent and would insure that at least this branch of the Congress would remain in close contact with the will of the people. In recent years there has been a great deal of discussion to the effect that congressional terms should be lengthened. Those who hold this view believe that a member of Congress is obliged to spend so much time campaigning that he or she does not have enough time to attend to the business of the national government.

This section also points out that to be an elector (voter) in a congressional election, one must abide by the qualifications set by the *state* for voting for state legislators. All qualified voters have a constitutionally protected right to cast their ballots and have them counted in a congressional election,[3] but both state and federal laws are involved. Each may make regulations on the same subject. The paramount character of those made by Congress, however, has the effect of superseding those made by the state if there is any inconsistency between them.[4] Various amendments to the Constitution and supplementary Acts of Congress passed immediately after the Civil War and in recent years insure that voters must be registered by the states without discrimination because of race, creed, color or sex, but even with such federal requirements, registration of voters and regulation of elections are still primarily state powers.

CLAUSE 2   There is a legal difference between being an "inhabitant" and a "legal resident" of a state, and it is interesting to note that the only requirement in the Constitution is that a candidate for Congress must be an inhabitant.

Students whose colleges are outside their home states remain legal residents of the states from which they came. They probably have drivers' licenses from their home states, are registered to vote at home and, when someone asks them where they are from, they give their home states. This and other criteria, such as an intention to remain there, make one a legal resident of a state. On the other hand, one is an inhabitant of a state in which one is physically present. The same student, while at school, is an inhabitant of the state where the college is located. The same rule applies to members of the Armed Forces stationed in the United States. They are legal residents of the state from which they came, but they are inhabitants of the state where they are stationed.

In 1964, Senator Robert F. Kennedy was elected to the Senate from New York, to which he had just moved, instead of from Massachusetts, where he had been a legal resident. Senator Kennedy was unable to vote in the election which he won since he had not been in New York long enough to satisfy the residency requirements for voter registration.

CLAUSE 3   "Direct taxes" are those imposed directly on property according to its value. "Other persons" meant slaves, and this clause has been obsolete since slavery was abolished. The entire bracketed portion of this clause was changed by Section 2 of the 14th Amendment.

The rest of this clause set up the original House of Representatives before the first census could be taken. If we had one Representative for every 30,000 people today, the House would be so enormous that no work could be done. Some years ago the House itself set its quota of members at 435, and that number of Representatives is distributed among the states on the basis of population, although all states have at least one Representative.

CLAUSE 4   This clause gives the governor of a state the authority to call a special election in case of the death or resignation of one of the state's Representatives.

CLAUSE 5   The Speaker of the House, the presiding officer of that body, is, as a matter of practice, chosen by the majority party.

When the House exercises its power of impeachment, it brings charges against a federal officer. In other words, the House acts in the same way that a grand jury acts in respect to an ordinary person accused of a crime. It issues a statement of charges against the official and presents the evidence of guilt to the Senate. House members do not determine the guilt or innocence of a person under impeachment. They only decide if the facts indicate a trial and present them to the Senate.

SECTION 3

1   The Senate of the United States shall be composed of two Senators from each State, [chosen by the Legislature thereof,] for six Years; and each Senator shall have one Vote.

2   Immediately after they shall be assembled in Consequence of the first Election, they shall be divided as equally as may be into three Classes. The Seats of the Senators of the first Class shall be vacated at the Expiration of the second Year, of the second Class at the Expiration of the fourth Year, and of the third Class at the Expiration of the sixth Year, so that one-third may be chosen every second Year; [and if Vacancies happen by Resignation, or otherwise, during the Recess of the Legislature of any State, the Executive thereof may make temporary Appointments until the next Meeting of the Legislature, which shall then fill such Vacancies.]

3   No Person shall be a Senator who shall not have attained to the Age of thirty Years, and been nine Years a Citizen of the United States,

and who shall not, when elected, be an Inhabitant of that State for which he shall be chosen.

4 The Vice President of the United States shall be President of the Senate, but shall have no Vote, unless they be equally divided.

5 The Senate shall chuse their other Officers, and also a President pro tempore, in the Absence of the Vice President, or when he shall exercise the Office of President of the United States.

6 The Senate shall have the sole Power to try all Impeachments. When sitting for that Purpose, they shall be on Oath or Affirmation. When the President of the United States is tried, the Chief Justice shall preside: And no Person shall be convicted without the Concurrence of two thirds of the Members present.

7 Judgment in Cases of Impeachment shall not extend further than to removal from Office, and disqualification to hold and enjoy any Office of honor, Trust or Profit under the United States: but the Party convicted shall nevertheless be liable and subject to Indictment, Trial, Judgment and Punishment, according to Law.

CLAUSE 1 The Senate is composed of two members from each state. At one time, the state legislatures elected Senators, but the 17th Amendment provided that the citizens of each state would elect Senators directly, just as they do members of the House of Representatives.

Unlike the House of Representatives, Senators serve for six years and only one-third of that body is elected in each general election. It is, therefore, a continuous body. This insures, or so the framers of the Constitution believed, a continuity of policy which we would not have if it were possible to elect entirely new members of both Houses of Congress in any one election.

CLAUSE 2 The bracketed portion of this clause was changed by the 17th Amendment. In case of a vacancy in the Senate, the governor of the state in which the vacancy occurs *appoints* someone to fill the unexpired term of the previous Senator. You will note that this differs from the procedure to be followed in case of a vacancy in the House of Representatives. However, the appointment only lasts until the next general election.

Example

Senator Y, from the State of New York, dies after a year of his senatorial term has passed. The Governor appoints X to his seat. X serves for another year, until the next general election. If he wishes to remain in the Senate, he must run for the remaining four years of the term.

An election to fill the remainder of a term is the only time it is possible for both Senate seats from the same state to be contested at the same time. The Senate is so composed that the terms for Senators from one state expire at different times, but in the case of an election to fill a vacancy, if the other Senator's term is regularly expiring at the same time, both seats will be contested in the same election.

CLAUSE 3 The same rules as to inhabitancy apply to the Senate as to the House.

CLAUSE 5 The President pro tempore (called the President pro tem) of the Senate is generally the Senator with the longest service.

CLAUSE 6 When a bill of impeachment which is similar to an indictment has been drawn by the House of Representatives, it is presented to the Senate, which exercises the same function as a jury in a criminal case. It hears the evidence against the impeached official, any evidence he wishes to present, considers the facts and finds the official guilty or not guilty. The Senate has the right to compel the attendance of witnesses and to require witnesses to answer in the same way that courts do. They must take an oath, as a juror does, to do their duty fairly and honestly.

CLAUSE 7 In all the history of our country, only five officials (all federal judges) have been impeached by the Senate. Fourteen bills of impeachment have been brought by the House. In 1974, for the second time in the history of our country, impeachment of a President became a possibility. The House Judiciary Committee voted three articles of impeachment against President Richard Nixon. When President Nixon resigned before the articles could be voted on by the full House, the proceedings where automatically terminated. The sole penalty which flows directly from an impeachment case is removal from office, and the Senate cannot send an impeached official to jail. However, the proper procedure would be to present the evidence on which the impeachment was based to the proper authorities in state or federal courts, who would then see that the official was tried under the ordinary criminal statutes by the ordinary processes of the law.

Example

Joe Blow, a federal judge, is suspected of taking a bribe from Ned Nasty, who was on trial in Blow's court and found not guilty. The House would investigate and if they decided there was reasonable cause to believe bribery had occurred, would issue a bill of impeachment and bring Blow to trial before the Senate. If the Senate found Blow guilty, he would be removed from office. The evidence would then go to the prosecutor in the federal courts of Blow's state, he would be indicted by a grand jury and tried in federal court. If convicted, only then would he go to jail.

SECTION 4

1 The Times, Places and Manner of holding Elections for Senators and Representatives, shall be prescribed in each State by the Legislature thereof; but the Congress may at any time by Law make or alter such Regulations, except as to the Place of Chusing Senators.

2 The Congress shall assemble at least once in every Year, and such Meeting shall [be on the first Monday in December,] unless they shall by Law appoint a different Day.

CLAUSE 1 Congress established the first Tuesday after the first Monday in November as election day. As we have already seen, Congress and the states have joint control of election practices and requirements, and this section, Amendments 14, 15, 17 and additional federal legislation have set the standards which Congress requires in federal elections.

CLAUSE 2 This clause has been superseded by Amendment 20.

SECTION 5

1 Each House shall be the Judge of the Elections, Returns and Qualifications of its own Members, and a Majority of each shall constitute a Quorum to do Business; but a smaller Number may adjourn from day to day, and may be authorized to compel the Attendance of absent Members, in such Manner, and under such Penalties as each House may provide.

2 Each House may determine the Rules of its Proceedings, punish its Members for disorderly Behavior, and with the Concurrence of two thirds, expel a Member.

3 Each House shall keep a Journal of its Proceedings, and from time to time publish the same, excepting such Parts as may in their Judgment require Secrecy; and the Yeas and Nays of the Members of either House on any question shall, at the Desire of one fifth of those Present, be entered on the Journal.

4 Neither House, during the Session of Congress, shall, without the Consent of the other, adjourn for more than three days, nor to any other Place than that in which the two Houses shall be sitting.

CLAUSE 1 Until 1969 the House and the Senate had the power to refuse to seat a duly elected representative who had come to sit in either House, and the courts had no power to intervene on behalf of a representative who had been refused his or her seat. However, on June 16, 1969 in an historic decision, the Supreme Court of the United States substantially restricted the power of either House of Congress to refuse to seat a duly elected member. Representative Adam Clayton Powell of New York had been denied his seat in the 90th Congress in 1967-68 as a result of his conviction of contempt of a New York court as well as alleged misappropriation of federal funds during the 89th Congress. In *Powell v. McCormack*[5] the Supreme Court interpreted Congress's power to judge "the qualifications of its members" to be restricted to a determination of those qualifications specifically set forth in Article I of the Constitution. In other words, it now appears that Congress can refuse to seat an elected member *only* if it finds that he or she does not meet the requirements of age, citizenship and inhabitancy which are stated in Article I, Section 2, Clause 2 for the House and Section 3, Clause 3 for the Senate. The Court stated, however, that once a member has been seated, the House of which he or she is a member may expel or discipline that member as it sees fit.

Either House may still exercise some control over the elections of its members. An incumbent Senator's re-election margin was so close that his opponent was entitled to a recount under state law. The Senator sought to enjoin the recount on the theory that this clause made the Senate the only body which could determine the outcome of the election. The Supreme Court held that the state had the authority to conduct a recount under its own law, since the Senate's authority to undertake an independent one if it wished to do so was not affected by any action the state might choose to take.[6]

Examples

1 Henry Horrid, a notorious gangster, is elected to the House of Representatives. The other members of the House are quite upset about this. Under the ruling in the *Powell* case, as long as Henry is 25, has been a citizen for 7 years and is an inhabitant of the state from which he was elected, he must be given the oath and allowed to take his seat. However, once this has been done, he may be expelled by a two-third vote of the House.

2 Yvette Youngster is only 23 when she is elected to the House. Since she does not meet the specific requirements for membership set forth in the Constitution, the House may, by a simple majority vote, deny her her seat.

Furthermore, the state has no power to refuse to send a duly elected representative to Washington.

Example

The Supreme Court of Maryland held that disqualification after election of a subversive person seeking to overthrow the federal government by force and violence must be determined by Congress itself and not by the state.[7]

CLAUSE 2 In addition to determining the rules of procedure for day-to-day activity on the floor of the House or Senate, members of the Congress also determine rules and procedures for committee hearings. A congressional committee may investigate in order to determine the necessity or advisability of future legislation, but it must set up rules before it begins and abide by them once the hearings have begun.[8] It may compel disclosures of facts relevant to its inquiry, but it has no constitutional power to expose witnesses or their associations simply for the sake of exposure.[9] A congressional committee is not required to give a witness all the rights which he would have in a federal criminal court.

A member of Congress is not subject to impeachment and the only method of expulsion, once seated, is by a two-thirds vote of a quorum (a majority) of the appropriate house.

SECTION 6

1 The Senators and Representatives shall receive a Compensation for their Services, to be ascertained by Law, and paid out of the Treasury of the United States. They shall in all Cases, except Treason, Felony and Breach of the Peace, be privileged from Arrest during their Attendance at the Session of their respective Houses, and in going to and returning from the same; and for any Speech or Debate in either House, they shall not be questioned in any other Place.

2 No Senator or Representative shall, during the Time for which he was elected, be appointed to any civil Office under the Authority of the United States, which shall have been created, or the Emoluments whereof shall have been encreased during such time; and no Person holding any Office under the United States, shall be a Member of either House during his Continuance in Office.

CLAUSE 1 Members of Congress are exempt from arrest in order to protect their independence in the legislature. At one time, a king could deal with dissident members of his legislature by arresting the rebels and holding them in jail until his measures had been passed by a more pliable parliament. It was in order to prevent any such interference that the framers of the Constitution inserted this clause. A member of Congress, however, is not exempt from civil suits or from a serious criminal charge, known as a "felony."

Examples

1   A Senator is driving to work one morning and violates the speed laws. She may be issued a ticket but she may not be arrested.

2   A Representative has a wreck on the way to work one morning and in due course, the other driver files a civil suit for damages against him. He is not privileged to ignore the suit.

3   A Representative commits murder. Murder is a felony. He may not plead privilege when he is arrested.

Three members of the Congress were involved in decisions involving Congressional immunity from criminal prosecution or investigation. The decision on whether or not immunity existed depended on the nature of the activities in which the Senators engaged.

A Congressman made a speech on the House floor in return for payment of money. His conviction was overturned when the Supreme Court held that any judicial inquiry into a Congressman's motivation for making a speech would be unconstitutional.[10]

A former Senator was charged with accepting bribes while in office. The bribes were paid him in exchange for his agreement to perform certain acts relating to nonlegislative Senate business. He claimed that since he had been a member of the Senate at the time the acts were supposed to have taken place, he was immune from criminal prosecution. The Supreme Court held that illegal political, as opposed to legislative, actions were not covered by the immunity provisions of this section. The former Senator could, therefore, be prosecuted.[11]

A Senator who opposed the government's actions in the Viet Nam conflict was given the Pentagon Papers when they were classified as "top secret." He convened the subcommittee of which he was chairman and read the Pentagon Papers to any member who wished to attend and allowed newsmen into the "hearing." He then placed all 47 volumes of the papers into the public record. Shortly thereafter, he made an agreement with a publishing company to publish the Pentagon Papers. A federal grand jury, investigating the conduct involved in transmission of the papers to unauthorized sources, subpoenaed the Senator's aide. They wished to ask him who had given the papers to the Senator. The Senator asked the Supreme Court to rule that his aide did not have to testify. The Court held that the immunity clause protected the Senator himself from being required to answer any questions about the subcommittee meeting and that the same protection must be given to his aide, since the aide was acting as the Senator's agent. However, the Court held that the grand jury could question the aide about non-legislative matters such as the Senator's arrangement with the publishing company, since that had nothing to do with his official business as a Senator.[12]

The fact that a member of Congress may not be sued for slander (oral defamation of character) for anything he or she says on the floor of Congress is a very important privilege. The basis of the rule of absolute immunity of congressional officials from damage done by their acts or speeches, even though it is *knowingly* false or wrong when it is done, is that the importance of the individual's hurt is overbalanced by the public necessity for untrammelled legislative activity.[13] A witness may not recover damages for any injury to his or her reputation which occurs in a congressional investigation.[14]

Examples

1 John Doe is a witness before a congressional committee and his appearance is televised. While he is testifying, a member of the committee makes the flat statement that Doe is a murderer. This is not true and the committee member knows it. Doe loses his job and all his friends. The member of the committee is not subject to suit.

2 The same Congressman, while addressing a club meeting, makes the same statement about Doe. Doe may file suit against him for slander and defamation of character.

There have been times in the history of our country, some quite recently, when wild accusations have been made in committees and innocent people badly hurt. However, were this power curbed, it is possible that members of Congress would be intimidated by fear of suit from carrying out proper investigations.

CLAUSE 2 No member of Congress may be a federal judge, act as a member of any part of the executive branch of the government (including the Cabinet) or hold an active commission in the Armed Forces while he or she is sitting in Congress.

SECTION 7

1 All Bills for raising Revenue shall originate in the House of Representatives; but the Senate may propose or concur with Amendments as on other Bills.

2 Every Bill which shall have passed the House of Representatives and the Senate, shall, before it become a Law, be presented to the President of the United States; If he approve he shall sign it, but if not he shall return it, with his Objections to that House in which it shall have originated, who shall enter the Objections at large on their Journal, and proceed to reconsider it. If after such Reconsideration two thirds of that House shall agree to pass the Bill, it shall be sent, together with the Objections, to the other House, by which it shall likewise be reconsidered, and if approved by two thirds of that House, it shall become a Law. But in all such Cases the Votes of both Houses shall be determined by Yeas and Nays, and the Names of the Persons voting for and against the Bill shall be entered on the Journal of each House respectively. If any Bill shall not be returned by the President within ten Days (Sundays excepted) after it shall have been presented to him, the Same shall be a Law, in like Manner as if he had signed it, unless the Congress by their Adjournment prevent its Return, in which Case it shall not be a Law.

3 Every Order, Resolution, or Vote to which the Concurrence of the Senate and House of Representatives may be necessary (except on a question of Adjournment) shall be presented to the President of the United States; and before the Same shall take Effect, shall be approved by him, or being disapproved by him, shall be repassed by two thirds of the Senate and House of Representatives, according to the Rules and Limitations prescribed in the Case of a Bill.

CLAUSE 2 This clause describes the procedure by which a bill becomes a law. A member in either house proposes a bill which goes to the appropriate committee (Judiciary, Armed Services, Foreign Relations, and the like) of the house of which he or she is a member. On many occasions identical bills are introduced into the Senate and House at the same time. When the committee under whose jurisdiction the bill falls has approved it by majority vote, it is submitted to the entire body for a vote. It then goes to the other house, where it is also considered by a committee and then considered by the entire body. The procedure in each house varies slightly. The House of Representatives has a Rules Committee to establish the conditions for debate of each bill before it is sent to the floor for debate by the full House. The Senate debates all bills under the same rules, so has no need for a Rules Committee.

If there is a difference in the versions passed by the House and Senate, the bill goes to a "conference committee" composed of members of both houses. Once the bill leaves that committee, it is repassed in identical form by both houses. It is then signed by the Speaker of the House and the President of the Senate and sent to the President.

The President may do one of three things to a bill. If he signs it, it becomes law. If he approves of the bill, but for political reasons does not wish to be responsible for it, he may exercise a "pocket veto." In this case, he keeps the bill but does not sign it. If Congress is still in session ten days after he receives the bill and he has not returned it, it becomes law without his signature. If, however, Congress has adjourned before the expiration of the ten days, the bill is dead. If the President vetoes the bill, he refuses to sign it and sends it back to Congress with his reasons. It may be sent back to the house in which it originated and if it is repassed by both houses with a two-thirds majority of a quorum, it becomes law without the President's signature and over his objections. The President must sign or veto the entire bill. He cannot accept part of it and reject other sections.

In order to allow Congress to legislate as well as to carry out its other responsibilities, it must have the authority to investigate. The power to investigate has become one of Congress's most used and sometimes abused powers. The power to investigate led to the development of the Congressional committee system. In recent years, almost any significant issue in American life and politics has been investigated by a Congressional committee, from whether or not one should be allowed to sell one's kidney for transplant to the activities of the National Security Council. Congress has used these broad powers to look into every major action of the President. This has led on many occasions to tension between the legislative and executive branches, and each is very protective of its powers.

In particular, Congress has tried to use its power to control the Executive branch through the "legislative veto." Congress delegates general powers to the Executive branch but may disapprove the plans for implementation. In *Immigration and Naturalization Service v. Chadha,*[15] a 1983 decision, the Supreme Court questioned the constitutionality of legislative vetoes. The full effects of this ruling are not yet clear, but Justice White wrote in dissent that the Court's decision "strikes down in one fell swoop provisions in more laws enacted by Congress than the Court has cumulatively invalidated in its history."

Example

The Clean Water Bill was passed almost without dissenting vote by both Houses of Congress in 1986 but was vetoed by President Ronald Reagan. As soon as the new Congress assembled in January, 1987, both Houses again passed the Bill. When President Reagan again vetoed it, both Houses then overrode his veto and the Clean Water Bill became law.

CLAUSE 3 This clause permits Congress to express its opinion on something which is not a proper subject for legislation. A concurrent resolution reflects the sentiment of both houses in matters such as the Gulf of Tonkin Resolution approving President Johnson's conduct of the Viet Nam conflict.

SECTION 8

Section 8 of Article I deals with specific powers of Congress. Except in the field of foreign relations, Congress has no powers except those specifically granted by some part of the Constitution or which may be implied from those specific grants. As you will see, the courts have taken a very broad view of what "may be implied" means, but in any case a federal law is unconstitutional unless it may be related to some power which Congress has.

By the nature of the federal system, the United States and not the individual states must carry out diplomatic business. Other countries do not send ambassadors to one of our states, they send them to the President, who represents the federal government. If the states carried on foreign relations, we would have no federal system and it is in the nature of our governmental system for Congress to legislate on the subject of foreign relations. The power to conduct foreign relations is therefore known as an "inherent power."

This section of Article I deals with enumerated powers of Congress. Congress also has powers which flow by implication from these enumerated powers, and which are necessary in order to carry out an enumerated power.

Example

Congress has an enumerated power to raise an army. From this may be implied the power to draft men for military service and to decide that women will not be drafted.[16]

1   The Congress shall have Power To lay and collect Taxes, Duties, Imposts and Excises, to pay the Debts and provide for the common Defence and general Welfare of the United States; but all Duties, Imposts and Excises shall be uniform throughout the United States;

2   To borrow Money on the credit of the United States;

3   To regulate Commerce with foreign Nations, and among the several States, and with the Indian Tribes;

4   To establish an uniform Rule of Naturalization, and uniform Laws on the subject of Bankruptcies throughout the United States;

5   To coin Money, regulate the Value thereof, and of foreign Coin, and fix the Standard of Weights and Measures;

6   To provide for the Punishment of counterfeiting the Securities and current Coin of the United States;

7   To establish Post Offices and post Roads;

8   To promote the Progress of Science and useful Arts, by securing for limited Times to Authors and Inventors the exclusive Right to their respective Writings and Discoveries;

9   To constitute Tribunals inferior to the supreme Court;

10   To define and punish Piracies and Felonies committed on the high Seas, and Offences against the Law of Nations;

11   To declare War, grant Letters of Marque and Reprisal, and make Rules concerning Captures on Land and Water;

12   To raise and support Armies, but no Appropriation of Money to that Use shall be for a longer Term than two Years;

13   To provide and maintain a Navy;

14   To make Rules for the Government and Regulation of the land and naval Forces;

15   To provide for calling forth the Militia to execute the Laws of the Union, suppress Insurrections and repel Invasions;

16   To provide for organizing, arming, and disciplining the Militia, and for governing such Part of them as may be employed in the Service of the United States, reserving to the States respectively, the Appointment of the Officers, and the Authority of training the Militia according to the discipline prescribed by Congress;

17 To exercise exclusive Legislation in all Cases whatsoever, over such District (not exceeding ten Miles square) as may, by Cession of particular States, and the Acceptance of Congress, become the Seat of the Government of the United States, and to exercise like Authority over all Places purchased by the Consent of the Legislature of the State in which the Same shall be, for the Erection of Forts, Magazines, Arsenals, dock-Yards, and other needful Buildings;—And

18 To make all Laws which shall be necessary and proper for carrying into Execution the foregoing Powers, and all other Powers vested by this Constitution in the Government of the United States, or in any Department or Officer thereof.

CLAUSE 1 Under our constitutional system, both national and state governments have the power to tax (dual power is known as "concurrent power"). The federal government may tax a *state's* activities if those activities are not part of the essential government of a state and are a profit-making enterprise.

Example

The State of New York bottled and sold mineral water. The courts held that such an activity was not an essential part of state government and as such was subject to federal taxation.[17]

Instrumentalities of the national government may not, however, be taxed by the states. This ruling was first enunciated by Chief Justice Marshall in the very famous case of *McCulloch v. Maryland*[18] in 1819. The Supreme Court still refuses to allow state taxation of any federal property, such as mail trucks, which do not bear state license tags since such are primarily revenue-raising devices, or federally owned real estate. The Supreme Court has held that a national bank was immune from state sales taxes on purchases made by the bank.[19]

This clause gives Congress the power to collect and levy taxes necessary for any purpose proper under any constitutional power.

The second portion of this clause prohibits duties which are not uniform at all ports.

Example

If you order a sweater from Scotland, the import duty would be the same if it arrived in the port of New York or the port of Charleston.

CLAUSE 2 This clause permits the government to issue savings bonds and paper money.

CLAUSE 3 This is the "interstate commerce" clause and is one of the most important congressional powers. The power of Congress to regulate commerce between the states is the power to enact all appropriate legislation for its protection and advancement.[20] Almost anything you eat or buy is in some way involved with interstate commerce. If you go to the movies, the film was probably sent from another state. If you eat in a restaurant, it is most unlikely that all the food and all the seasoning and all the silverware came from within your state. If you buy something in a store, it probably came from the factory across a state line. All transportation industries are part of interstate commerce.

As you can see, in modern-day America it is virtually impossible to exist without encountering interstate commerce. Where it goes, Congress has the power to regulate it.

Examples

1 Under this clause, Congress was empowered by the 1964 Civil Rights Act to prohibit racial discrimination in public eating establishments.

2 Labor-management relations are, in the main, regulated by federal law under this clause.

There is another aspect of this problem which should be noted, which is the power of the states to make laws regarding these subjects. In general, where there has been only partial exercise by the federal government of its power to regulate interstate commerce, the state may legislate on the phases which have been left unregulated, but when the United States exercises its legislative power so as to conflict with state regulation, the state law usually becomes inoperative and the federal legislation is exclusive in its application.[21] This power of the federal government is called "pre-emption."

If a local or state statute or regulation is more stringent than a federal one, however, preemption may not occur. For example,[22] federal regulations governing blood plasma centers do not preempt more stringent county regulations. Thus a state may set a higher standard than the federal government does, but not a lower one. Most areas of labor-management relations, for example, fall into areas which have been pre-empted by federal legislation. Most areas of labor-management relations, for example, fall into areas which have been pre-empted by federal legislation.

As you can see, Congress has the constitutional power to interject federal legislation into virtually every aspect of all commerce. Whether it should or should not exercise this power is another question, the answer to which depends on your view of the role of the federal government, but it does, quite clearly, have this power if it chooses to use it.

CLAUSE 4 The naturalization clause permits Congress to do two things. It may legislate on the subject of the admission of immigrants to this country and it may legislate on the requirements for naturalization. A "naturalized citizen" is one who was born a citizen of another country and becomes a citizen of the United States by following certain procedures set forth by federal law. Also, this clause gives Congress, by implication, the power to revoke citizenship for a naturalized citizen who has committed certain specific criminal offenses against the United States government. In effect, there are only two differences between the rights of the native-born American citizen and a naturalized citizen. A naturalized citizen is ineligible to become President of the United States and a naturalized citizen may have his citizenship revoked. A native-born American may renounce his citizenship but it may not be revoked against his will.[23]

Bankruptcy laws belong, because of this clause, exclusively in the domain of federal law. A bankrupt person is one who owes more money than he has assets. He may wish to go into voluntary bankruptcy in order to discharge finally these debts or his creditors may throw him into involuntary bankruptcy. The debtor must declare all his assets and the creditors appear and list the debts and the final result is that the creditors are paid a certain percentage of what is owed them and the bankrupt person is discharged from further liability. He is, however, still liable for such debts as alimony payments.

Courts created by Congress, however, must conform to the requirements of Article III. In 1978, Congress enacted the Bankruptcy Reform Act[24] which provided for new bankruptcy judges. The judges would serve fourteen year terms and could be removed for incompetence. In 1982 the Supreme Court held that the Act violated Article III of the Constitution which provides that all federal judges have life tenure and that their salaries cannot be reduced.[25]

CLAUSE 8 Congress has the power to issue patents to protect an inventor's right in his invention, although to qualify for a patent, the invention must be new and useful. After a patent has been issued, no one may use the device without the permission and payment of royalties to the patentee. Similarly, a writer may get a copyright on a book, a play, a movie, or music, which prohibits others from using what he has created without acknowledging his authorship and payment of a royalty.

Patent and copyright cases now involve topics of which the men who wrote the Constitution would never have dreamed.[26] Is computer software subject to patent or copyright regulation? Is a computer program an invention or creative writing? For example, the Supreme Court held in 1984 that the sale of home videocassette recorders did not infringe the copyrights of television programs.[27]

CLAUSE 9 All federal courts, the subject of Article III, except the Supreme Court, are established and may be abolished by Congress.

CLAUSE 10 Effective use of this clause is difficult because there is no definite code of international law. However, it permits Congress to enact federal laws which make murder or other crimes on the high seas a crime against the government of the United States *as long as* they are committed on United States ships.

CLAUSE 11 Letters of Marque and Reprisal, banned by international agreement in 1856, were issued by a government to private individuals and gave them power to raid enemy shipping without being guilty of piracy.

This clause makes it quite clear that Congress is the proper branch of the government for declaring war and establishing programs necessary for pursuing it. This involves the rule that in wartime, the rights of the individual must yield to the face of necessity and to the extent necessary for the preservation of the state.[28] The war power is the power to wage war successfully and one which permits harnessing of the entire efforts of the people. Congress may, therefore, in time of war, require rationing and price controls. However, the direct interference with liberty and property and abridgement of constitutional guarantees of freedom can be justified only when the danger to the government is real and impending.[29]

The last time Congress declared war was at the beginning of World War II. All military actions by the Armed Forces of the United States since the close of that war have not been "wars" in the legal sense. The President, as commander-in-chief of the troops, has dispatched them to Korea, Vietnam and other trouble spots without a declaration of war. He is empowered to do this under Article II. This power of the President has been the subject of a great deal of congressional dissatisfaction in the course of the Vietnam conflict and since that time. On the other hand, with present-day weapons on the world scene, an attack upon the United States would require instant dispatch of men and weapons and the President would have no time to request Congress to assemble and issue a declaration of war before retaliation could take place.

In 1973, Congress passed the War Powers Resolution to define and limit Presidential power to dispatch the military. To a great degree, however, the Resolution has been ineffective.

CLAUSE 12   This clause gives Congress the power of the purse over the military. The President may send troops as he pleases, but if Congress disapproves, it does not have to issue the money to pay them until he brings them home. This clause also permits Congress, by implication, to establish the draft. The two-year restriction on appropriations was designed to insure the civilian supremacy over the military, a cornerstone of the Anglo-Saxon and American legal systems.

CLAUSE 13   The Navy is likewise established and financed by Congress.

CLAUSE 15   The "Militia" in the Constitution refers to what we know as the National Guard. Until it is "federalized" the Guard is a state-supervised organization, but the President and the Congress may call it up into federal service in case of emergency, at which time it becomes a part of the Army. As a result of legislation by Congress delegating its power to him, the President may call up the Guard without consulting Congress, should the need arise.

CLAUSE 16   Although the Guard is a state organization, Congress appropriates money for it and may control it through appropriation.

CLAUSE 17   Congress has exclusive jurisdiction over all federal property. An Armed Forces base in the United States is federal territory, and any crimes committed by civilians thereon are tried in federal court, although the state may exercise concurrent jurisdiction in some respects.

Until 1973, the District of Columbia was governed by a Congressional committee and those local officials appointed by that committee. A citizen of the District had no voice in local affairs. The "Home Rule" statute allowed election of a mayor and other officials who handle all local matters in the same way the mayor and other officials operate any other city. Congress still maintains the streets and provides for fire and police protection for the area of the District encompassing federal monuments and buildings.

CLAUSE 18   This clause gives Congress the power to make all laws which are necessary to execute its powers granted by the Constitution or to facilitate the exercise of powers given to the President or the judiciary. However, the term "necessary" includes all appropriate means which are conducive to the end to be accomplished. "Proper" means "convenient."[30] It does *not* mean that Congress has the power to exercise any function which it chooses although there is no constitutional basis for such.

SECTION 9

There are certain specified acts which the Constitution expressly prohibits to Congress. These are enumerated in Section 9.

1   The Migration or Importation of such Persons as any of the States now existing shall think proper to admit, shall not be prohibited by the Congress prior to the Year one thousand eight hundred and eight, but a Tax or duty may be imposed on such Importation, not exceeding ten dollars for each Person.

2　The Privilege of the Writ of Habeas Corpus shall not be suspended, unless when in Cases of Rebellion or Invasion the public Safety may require it.

3　No Bill of Attainder or ex post facto Law shall be passed.

4　No Capitation, or other direct, Tax shall be laid, unless in Proportion to the Census or Enumeration herein before directed to be taken.

5　No Tax or Duty shall be laid on Articles exported from any State.

6　No Preference shall be given by any Regulation of Commerce or Revenue to the Ports of one State over those of another: nor shall Vessels bound to, or from, one State, be obliged to enter, clear, or pay Duties in another.

7　No Money shall be drawn from the Treasury, but in Consequence of Appropriations made by Law; and a regular Statement and Account of the Receipts and Expenditures of all public Money shall be published from time to time.

8　No Title of Nobility shall be granted by the United States: And no Person holding any Office of Profit or Trust under them, shall, without the Consent of the Congress, accept of any present, Emolument, Office, or Title, of any kind whatever, from any King, Prince, or foreign State.

CLAUSE 1　This clause referred to the slave trade and is therefore now obsolete.

CLAUSE 2　This clause guarantees one of the most important rights a citizen of the United States can have. "Habeas corpus" means, in Latin, "you have the body" and writs are issued to bring a party in custody before a judge. It is concerned with the legality of the detention and not with the guilt or innocence of the accused if he is charged with a proper crime. Every person, regardless of where he is held, whose liberty has been unlawfully restrained, has an absolute right to test the legality of his detention by use of this writ.[31] Habeas corpus is also the appropriate remedy for a prisoner who is denied the effective assistance of counsel.[32]

If you are in jail and wish to get out, your lawyer would ask a judge to issue a writ of habeas corpus. You and the sheriff or the person who has you in custody would be brought before the judge. The judge would then determine (1) if you were held on a legitimate criminal charge and (2) whether bail should be granted. If the jailor can show that you are properly in custody, the judge will not grant the writ. The judge does not determine whether or not you are guilty of the crime as charged. He merely determines if you are charged with a legitimate crime.

Examples

1　A man is brought before a judge on a writ of habeas corpus and the jailor testifies that the man is being held on a charge of car theft, that bail had been set and that the man could not pay it. The judge determines that the man is being held on a valid charge and denies the writ.

2　A man is brought before the judge on a writ and the jailor testifies that he is being held because he has red hair. The judge would decide that there is no criminal offense charged and order the man released.

Writs of habeas corpus are also issued in noncriminal cases in which a person wishes to get out of a place of confinement.

Example

Mr. A's wife has him committed to a state mental hospital and he is not allowed to leave. He maintains that he is not in need of treatment. He applies for a writ of habeas corpus. At the hearing, the judge hears testimony from the hospital officials as to Mr. A's condition. If the judge finds that Mr. A is being held for good medical reasons, he may deny the writ, but if Mr. A is being held without just medical cause, the writ will be issued and Mr. A will be able to leave the hospital.[33]

There are times when the national interest in time of war requires suspension of the writ of habeas corpus. It may be suspended for enemy aliens, who are usually interned until the cessation of hostilities.[34] During World War II, many native-born Americans of Japanese ancestry were interned as security risks in camps set up by the federal government. Although denial of their right of habeas corpus was upheld by the courts,[35] it is doubtful that such wholesale internments would again be permitted. Even in times of national emergency, when the government has the power to confine a person indefinitely and without bringing charges against him, obvious dangers to basic freedoms have occurred.

CLAUSE 3   A bill of attainder is a legislative act passed against a named person pronouncing him guilty of a crime without a trial.

Example

The Congress passes a law saying Joe Blow is a thief, and that he will be sentenced to 10 years in the federal penitentiary.

Since it is the business of the judicial branch of the government to determine guilt or innocence of criminal acts and the business of the legislative branch to specify behavior, not individuals, as criminal, bills of attainder are forbidden.

An ex post facto law is one which imposes punishment for an act which was not punishable at the time it was committed or which imposes additional punishment. A retroactive law which does not impose a criminal penalty is not an ex post facto law and does not violate this provision of the Constitution.

Example

If it is perfectly legal today to ship firearms in interstate commerce, Congress may not make it a criminal act next week and punish you for having shipped two rifles this morning.

In 1984, the Supreme Court held that a federal statute requiring compliance with draft registration in order for a college student to be eligible for federal financial aid was not a bill of attainder.[36] The statute did not single out an identifiable group and there was no punishment.

CLAUSE 4   This clause has been modified by the 16th Amendment which permits the levying of income taxes and is no longer of use. A direct tax is one on real or personal property by reason of its being owned by the taxpayer.

CLAUSE 5   You may not be required to pay a duty on an article which you send to another country.

CLAUSE 6   Import duties must be the same at all ports.

CLAUSE 7   This clause gives Congress the power of the purse-strings over all aspects of the federal government's activities. It is a restriction upon the power of the executive department to spend, and means simply that no money can be paid out of the Treasury unless it has been appropriated by an act of Congress. This gives final approval of all governmental activity to the legislative branch.

CLAUSE 8   The United States is prohibited from creating a class of peers as was found in England and from granting such titles as Duke, Earl, and so forth.

SECTION 10

This section prohibits states from carrying on certain specified activities. In addition to these prohibitions, of course, as we saw in the section on interstate commerce, because of the principle of the supremacy of federal law found in Article VI, the federal government may restrict the operation of state laws by implication by the passage of conflicting federal laws.

1   No State shall enter into any Treaty, Alliance, or Confederation; grant Letters of Marque and Reprisal; coin Money; emit Bills of Credit; make any Thing but gold and silver Coin a Tender in Payment of Debts; pass any Bill of Attainder, ex post facto Law, or Law impairing the Obligation of Contracts, or grant any Title of Nobility.

2   No State shall, without the Consent of the Congress, lay any Imposts or Duties on Imports or Exports, except what may be absolutely

necessary for executing its inspection Laws: and the net Produce of all Duties and Imposts, laid by any State on Imports or Exports, shall be for the Use of the Treasury of the United States; and all such Laws shall be subject to the Revision and Controul of the Congress.

3 No State shall, without the Consent of Congress, lay any duty of Tonnage, keep Troops, or Ships of War in time of Peace, enter into any Agreement or Compact with another State, or with a foreign Power, or engage in War, unless actually invaded, or in such imminent Danger as will not admit of delay.

CLAUSE 1 A state would obviously destroy the fundamental system of our government if it made a treaty with a foreign nation. To do so would render the existence of the national government unimportant.

A "bill of credit" is paper (which will be redeemed at a later date) issued to be used as money.

A state law which impairs the obligation of a contract is one which alters the legal duty of the parties to abide by an agreement which, at the time it was made, the law recognized as enforceable.

Example

The legal rate of interest in Mr. Doodle Bugg's state is 10%. Mr. Bugg borrows money at that rate on Monday. On Tuesday, the state legislature makes a law that the legal rate is 6%. If Mr. Bugg were permitted to go to court and ask to have the interest on his note reduced, the state would have impaired the obligation of his contract.

CLAUSE 2 No state may charge an export duty for goods going out of state or an import duty on goods shipped from out of the country or from another state. However, inspections of incoming goods may be required to protect the health of the citizens. As long as the amount of inspection fee charged is merely to defray expenses, the fee is not unconstitutional.[37]

Examples

1 Some states require inspection of fruit brought from another state in order to control Japanese beetles. A small fee in order to pay expenses of such inspection is valid.

2 A statute providing for the inspection of oil products which required the payment of a fee per barrel to defray expenses did not violate this clause.

3 A fee charged on books shipped into the state would be unconstitutional.

CLAUSE 3 A "duty of tonnage" is a fee charged to a vessel before it may enter the ports of a state.

This clause also prohibits states from having their own armies which are not subject to federal regulation.

States are not required to obtain congressional approval to join in a "reciprocity statute."[38] A reciprocity statute is one made by two or more states in which each one gives citizens of the other certain privileges on condition that its citizens enjoy the same privileges while in the other states.

Example

The Uniform Support of Dependents Act has been adopted by most states. If a man deserts his family in New York and moves to California, normal court procedures would require that he be brought back to New York for trial on the question of alimony and child support. This usually takes a great deal of time and in the meantime, the family could suffer severe hardship. The Uniform Act provides that the facts would be sent to a California judge by a New York court, the judge in California would determine the amount of support to be paid and the California court would collect the money and send it to the New York court for distribution to the family. The New York courts would do the same for a California man who had abandoned his family in California.

On the other hand, an agreement between two states regarding joint land use would require congressional approval.

Example

Agreements on the use of hydroelectric power by states located on a river which ran among them would be a "compact" and would require congressional approval. [39]

Article Two

ARTICLE II deals with the executive branch of the government—the President of the United States—and specifies his powers, duties, responsibilities and qualifications for office. He has no powers not derived from the Constitution.[1] It is his responsibility, first and foremost, to carry out the laws which have been made by the legislative branch.

The men who wrote the Constitution probably had no idea that the President of the United States would ever exert as much power as present-day Presidents do. The Executive Branch now initiates legislation and is responsible for activities of the governmental departments to which he has delegated some of his powers. The American President is now not only the most powerful individual in our own country, but is one of the most powerful people in the entire world. This growth of the President's power is an excellent example of the ways in which our constitutional government has grown and changed by custom and usage.

SECTION 1

1 The executive Power shall be vested in a President of the United States of America. He shall hold his Office during the Term of four Years, and, together with the Vice-President, chosen for the same Term, be elected, as follows

2 Each State shall appoint, in such Manner as the Legislature thereof may direct, a Number of Electors, equal to the whole Number of Senators and Representatives to which the State may be entitled in the Congress: but no Senator or Representative, or Person holding an Office of Trust or Profit under the United States, shall be appointed an Elector. [The Electors shall meet in their respective States, and vote by Ballot for two persons, of whom one at least shall not be an Inhabitant of the same State with themselves. And they shall make a List of all the Persons voted for, and of the Number of Votes for each; which List they shall sign and certify, and transmit sealed to the Seat of the Government of the United States, directed to the President of the Senate. The President of the Senate shall, in the Presence of the Senate and House of Representatives, open all the Certificates, and the Votes shall then be counted. The Person having the greatest Number of Votes shall be the President, if such Number be a Majority of the whole Number of Electors appointed; and if there be more than one who have such Majority, and have an equal Number of Votes, then the House of Representatives shall immediately chuse by Ballot one of them for President; and if no Person have a Majority, then from the five highest on the List the said House shall in like Manner chuse the President. But in chusing the President, the Votes shall be taken by States, the Representation from each State having one Vote; A quorum for this Purpose shall consist of a Member or Members from two-thirds of the States, and

a Majority of all the States shall be necessary to a Choice. In every Case, after the Choice of the President, the Person having the greatest Number of Votes of the Electors shall be the Vice President. But if there should remain two or more who have equal Votes, the Senate Shall chuse from them by Ballot the Vice President.]

3 The Congress may determine the Time of chusing the Electors, and the Day on which they shall give their Votes; which Day shall be the same throughout the United States.

4 No Person except a natural born Citizen, or a Citizen of the United States, at the time of the Adoption of this Constitution, shall be eligible to the Office of President; neither shall any Person be eligible to that Office who shall not have attained to the Age of thirty-five Years, and been fourteen Years a Resident within the United States.

5 In Case of the Removal of the President from Office, or of his Death, Resignation, or Inability to discharge the Powers and Duties of the said Office, the same shall devolve on the Vice President, and the Congress may by Law provide for the Case of Removal, Death, Resignation or Inability, both of the President and Vice President, declaring what Officer shall then act as President, and such Officer shall act accordingly, until the Disability be removed, or a President shall be elected.

6 The President shall, at stated Times, receive for his Services, a Compensation, which shall neither be increased nor diminished during the Period for which he shall have been elected, and he shall not receive within that Period any other Emolument from the United States, or any of them.

7 Before he enter on the Execution of his Office, he shall take the following Oath or Affirmation:—"I do solemnly swear (or affirm) that I will faithfully execute the Office of President of the United States, and will to the best of my Ability, preserve, protect and defend the Constitution of the United States."

CLAUSE 1 Although not specifically mentioned in the Constitution, the doctrine of Executive Privilege, the power of the President to withhold information from Congress, had been accepted until the time of the Watergate scandals. When Alexander Butterfield, a Presidential aide, told the Select Committee investigating Nixon's role in the matter that President Nixon tape recorded all conversations in his office, the Committee demanded the tapes. Nixon refused to release them and the matter ended in the Supreme Court. In *United States v. Nixon*,[2] the Court recognized the proper role of executive privilege but declared that when challenged, the burden was on the White House to prove a need to protect diplomatic or military secrets and specifical-

ly excluded from it any evidence of criminal wrongdoing in the White House.

The President is absolutely immune from any damage awards in suits brought against him for any activity involving his Presidency, even if a court eventually decides that the presidential action that was the subject of the suit violated the plaintiff's rights.[3] Presidential aides, however, have only qualified immunity in this situation.[4]

CLAUSE 2 The method of election of the President will be discussed under Amendment 12. It is sufficient to say here that the President and Vice President are only indirectly elected by the voters. The second portion of this clause has been entirely superseded by Amendment 12.

CLAUSE 3 As we have seen, Congress has chosen the Tuesday after the first Monday in November as election day.

CLAUSE 4 The office of President of the United States is the only one which a naturalized citizen may not hold. A candidate born of American parents in a foreign country would be considered to be a native-born American and is eligible for election as long as he has complied with the fourteen-year residency requirement. Senator Barry Goldwater, Republican candidate for President in 1964, was born in Arizona when it was still a territory and, of course, was an American citizen by birth.

CLAUSE 5 The problem of an incapacitated President has been one of the more serious constitutional problems in our history and the 25th Amendment was adopted in order to deal with it. When a President dies in office, the Vice President succeeds him and assumes the title and the responsibilities of President. The question of whether a Vice President actually became President or was merely an Acting President was settled in 1841 when Tyler became President and set a precedent for future Vice Presidents to follow. The difficulties arise, however, when a President is too ill to carry out his duties but the office has not been vacated. President Wilson's illness in 1919 and 1920 is the best example of prolonged incapacitation. Until quite recently, this question was never settled and there have been times when the office of the President was virtually unoccupied. Beginning with President Eisenhower and continuing through Presidents Kennedy and Johnson, each man made an agreement with his Vice President as to the circumstances under which the Vice President would assume control of Presidential duties. However, these agreements were merely stop-gap arrangements, had no legal force, and obviously were not sufficient.

The problem would arise most critically in the event that a President ever became mentally ill or senile. A President who has had a heart attack normally realizes he is too sick to act and is aware of the necessity of relinquishing his duties. However, in some forms of mental disease or senility, the nature of the difficulty would be such that the President would not voluntarily give up his responsibilities and powers. The 25th Amendment provides for involuntary removal of the President from his power (but not from his office) if this tragedy should ever occur.

CLAUSE 6 If Congress were able to reduce the Presidential salary, they could starve him out of office if they did not approve of his administration.

CLAUSE 7 Any judicial officer, including a justice of the peace, may administer the Presidential oath. When President Lyndon Johnson was sworn in following the assassination of President Kennedy, the oath was administered by a woman, Judge Sarah T. Hughes of the Federal District Court.

The President becomes President when his term begins or, if he succeeds from the Vice-Presidency, when the previous President dies. His office is not assumed from the time he takes the oath.

Example

President Johnson became President at the instant President Kennedy died. The office was not vacant between the President's death and administration of the oath to President Johnson.

SECTION 2

1 The President shall be Commander in Chief of the Army and Navy of the United States, and of the Militia of the several States, when called into the actual Service of the United States; he may require the Opinion in writing, of the principal Officer in each of the executive Departments, upon any subject relating to the Duties of their respective Offices, and he shall have Power to Grant Reprieves and Pardons for Offenses against the United States, except in Cases of Impeachment.

2 He shall have Power, by and with the Advice and Consent of the Senate, to make Treaties, provided two-thirds of the Senators present concur; and he shall nominate, and by and with the Advice and Consent of the Senate, shall appoint Ambassadors, other public

Ministers and Consuls, Judges of the supreme Court, and all other Officers of the United States, whose Appointments are not herein otherwise provided for, and which shall be established by Law: but the Congress may by Law vest the Appointment of such inferior Officers, as they think proper, in the President alone, in the Courts of Law, or in the Heads of Departments.

3 The President shall have Power to fill up all Vacancies that may happen during the Recess of the Senate, by granting Commissions which shall expire at the End of their next Session.

CLAUSE 1 This clause invests the President with the right to wage a war which the Congress has declared and to carry into effect all laws passed by Congress for the conduct of war and for the government and regulation of the Armed Forces.[5] The President also has the authority to dispatch troops throughout the world without waiting for a congressional declaration of war. In fact, Congress has only declared war five times in our history, while American troops have fought outside the United States more than 150 times. Our Founding Fathers feared the military establishment so they quite clearly made a civilian the supreme commander.

Although the Cabinet is not mentioned anywhere in the Constitution, the drafters of the Constitution realized the obvious need for executive departments and assumed that they would exist. The Departments of State, War and the Treasury were established in 1789.

The President may reprieve or pardon any criminal who has committed a *federal* crime. A pardon, in effect, wipes away the criminal record. It restores all civil rights and releases the offender from all disabilities, such as a sentence of imprisonment, imposed by the offense. It does not, however, impose upon the government any obligation to compensate the offender for anything he may have suffered by reason of his imprisonment.[6] A reprieve merely postpones the execution of the sentence. A President is powerless to pardon a criminal convicted of a *state* crime.[7]

Examples

1 Mr. Bad Mann throws a rock through the Post Office window. This is a federal crime. He is tried, convicted and sentenced to a term of imprisonment in the federal penitentiary. The President may pardon or reprieve him.

2 Luke Looped is tried, convicted and sentenced for drunk driving in a state court and is serving his term in the state penitentiary. The President

may not pardon or reprieve him, but the governor of the state has the power to do so.

After President Nixon resigned, President Ford, citing as his reason a desire to let the nation heal from the wounds of Watergate and to get on to other unsolved national problems, unconditionally pardoned Nixon, even though he had not been indicted for any crime.[8] The pardon created such a national uproar that it was an important factor in President Ford's loss of the next election to Jimmy Carter.

CLAUSE 2 A treaty is a compact made between two or more nations. Because a treaty becomes part of the federal law, a state law which conflicts with it must yield to the treaty.[9] As a matter of practice, instead of asking for Senatorial advice, the President and his representatives negotiate treaties and then ask the Senate for ratification. Ratification must be by a two-thirds vote of a quorum of 51 Senators. In recent years, most of the treaties which the Presidents have signed have been ratified, but some of them have not been assured of overwhelming support. Although President Wilson was largely responsible for the drafting of the Charter of the League of Nations, the Senate refused to ratify it.

The Senate has also never ratified the Strategic Arms Limitation Treaty (SALT II) between the United States and the Soviet Union.

The Constitution is silent about terminating treaties. In 1979 President Carter announced the termination of the treaty between this country and Taiwan. He did this without obtaining Congressional approval. Senator Barry Goldwater challenged President Carter's action in court, but the Supreme Court upheld the President.[10]

The President has sidestepped the consent right of the Senate by using executive agreements. Executive agreements are negotiated by the State Department and validated by the President. From 1973 to the beginning of 1987, the United States entered into 157 treaties and 3,296 executive agreements.

Only a majority vote is required to confirm a Presidential appointment. The "vacancies" referred to in Clause 3 refer to the list given in Clause 2.

CLAUSE 3 During a recess of the Senate, the President has the power to fill, by temporary commission, a vacancy which occurred during the previous session. A temporary commission continues until the end of the next session of Congress.

Example

The President appoints his son-in-law as Ambassador to Great Britain during a recess of the Congress. When Congress comes back into its new session, the Senate unanimously refuses to confirm the appointment. The Ambassador remains on his post until the end of the session.

SECTION 3

He shall from time to time give to the Congress Information of the State of the Union, and recommend to their Consideration such Measures as he shall judge necessary and expedient; he may, on extraordinary Occasions, convene both Houses, or either of them, and in Case of Disagreement between them, with Respect to the Time of Adjournment, he may adjourn them to such Time as he shall think proper; he shall receive Ambassadors and other public Ministers; he shall take Care that the Laws be faithfully executed, and shall Commission all the Officers of the United States.

Each year the President must present, in person or otherwise, a "State of the Union" message to Congress in which he reviews national progress during the preceding year and presents, in general terms, his plans for the next year.

The duty of the President to see that the laws are faithfully executed is not limited to the enforcement of Acts of Congress, but includes the rights, duties and obligations growing out of the Constitution, our international relations and all the protections to citizens implied by the nature of the government under the Constitution.[11]

The President commissions, among others, all officers in the Armed Forces.

SECTION 4

The President, Vice President and all civil Officers of the United States, shall be removed from Office on Impeachment for, and Conviction of, Treason, Bribery, or other high Crimes and Misdemeanors.

All civil officers of the federal government may be impeached. This excludes military officers and members of Congress. As we have seen, impeachment extends only to removal from office, but ordinary proceedings in federal or state criminal courts may follow.

The grounds for impeachment are only that of commission of a crime and not because a majority of the Congress thinks the President or judge involved is of obnoxious political beliefs or has in good faith mismanaged his office. Senility, inability to function for any reason or other difficulties which do not constitute a criminal offense are not grounds for impeachment. An offense charged in an impeachment must be a criminal act which implies moral turpitude (conduct contrary to justice, honesty or good morals), which is dangerous to the safety of the state, and which makes an incumbent unfit to remain in his office.[12]

The House Judiciary Committee voted three articles of impeachment against President Richard M. Nixon. Article I charged him with criminal obstruction of justice during the investigations of the Watergate scandal. Article II charged him with criminal violations of the rights of American citizens, alleging his complicity in the Watergate break-ins and wiretaps. Article III charged him with refusing to provide the Congressional investigators with tape recordings and records they had subpoenaed. Mr. Nixon resigned before the full House of Representatives voted to send the Bill of Impeachment to the Senate.

Examples

1 If Joseph Blow, President of the United States, accepts a bribe to veto a bill, he has committed a federal crime. He may be impeached.

2 If Joseph Blow, President of the United States, dresses himself in a toga and goes to Congress and tells them he is Emperor Julius Caesar reincarnated, he may not be impeached. Since the adoption of Amendment 25, Blow's powers would probably be given to the Vice President until he recovered.

Article Three

ARTICLE III deals with the third branch of the government—the judicial branch. The Supreme Court is established by this Article and, as we have seen, by Article I, but all lower federal courts and the jurisdiction of all federal courts including the Supreme Court, have been established by Congress and may be altered or abolished by it.

Courts have what is known as "judicial power." This means they may decide cases which are actually before them and pronounce judgment between the parties to the case. They may not decide hypothetical questions and they have no investigative power.

Alone among the court systems of the world, state and federal courts in the United States exercise a most important power known as "judicial review." There is no mention of judicial review in the Constitution because it grew as a matter of practice and not constitutional or statutory directive. Judicial review is the power of a court to declare a law or act of the executive unconstitutional—that is, to determine the validity of the law or act in relation to the higher constitutional law which binds all branches of the government.

Since they have the power of judicial review, the courts are, in effect, the most powerful of the three branches of government. The federal courts may declare Acts of Congress, actions of the President or any part of the executive branch, state statutes and state court decisions to be in conflict with the Constitution and therefore void. As a matter of fact, most determinations of constitutionality in the Supreme Court involve decisions made by state courts on state laws.

Since it is a grave matter to superimpose the decision of nine persons upon the actions of the elected legislative branch of the government, the Supreme Court has made rules to guide itself and the lower federal courts in determining constitutional cases. In the first place, a real case with damage to a real party must be presented. The Court will neither answer hypothetical questions nor offer advice to anyone, including Congress and the President. The person asking the Court to declare unconstitutional a statute or lower court decision must show that he has actually been damaged by the unconstitutionality.[1] Most important of all, if there is any possibility of construing a statute so as to render it constitutional, the courts must do it.

The organization of the federal court system has been established by Congress. The Supreme Court, which sits in Washington and consists of nine justices, is, of course, the highest court. There are 12 Circuit Courts of Appeal scattered throughout the country and there are 94 federal District Courts. Congress frequently increases the number of District Courts in order to keep up with the volume of cases and reduce the length of time parties must wait to have their cases heard.

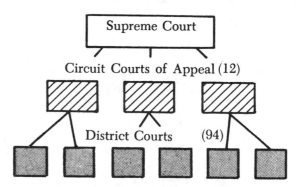

In addition to the system of federal courts, of course all states have court systems. There are state trial courts and state appellate courts usually known as supreme courts, and, in some cases, intermediate courts of appeal.

The federal District Court is the first or lowest federal court. It is here that juries hear and determine the guilt of defendants charged with a federal crime. It is here that damages are awarded or denied by juries in civil actions.

Examples

1 You are involved in a collision with a driver from another state and sue him in federal court. The jury in federal District Court will hear the

evidence and either award damages to you or determine that the other driver was not guilty of negligence.

2 You throw a brick through a post office window. Since this is federal property, you have violated a federal criminal law. You are tried in federal District Court by a jury and found guilty or not guilty.

Appeals from the District Court go to the Circuit Court of Appeals, but only on matters of law. The jury is the final determiner of the facts (whether or not you threw the brick through the window) and the appeals court hears appeals only on questions involving the law (whether or not there is a criminal statute prohibiting throwing bricks through post office windows). Further appeals would go to the United States Supreme Court. It is very important to note that one may, if a federal question is presented, appeal from the decision of a state supreme court but not from any lower state courts.

Since Congress has the right to fix the jurisdiction of all federal courts, it has established certain requirements before the Supreme Court may hear a case. In some instances, there is a right to have a case heard by the Supreme Court. This is called an "appeal," which is used in a very technical sense in this case.

Appeals to the United States Supreme Court can be made from three types of lower court:

FEDERAL DISTRICT COURTS

a When a federal statute has been held unconstitutional,[2] provided the United States or one of its employees is a party to the suit.

Examples

1 Congress passes a law making it a crime to have red hair. You are arrested and brought before the district court for trial. The judge holds the statute unconstitutional. The government may appeal to the Supreme Court. The court *must* hear the case.

2 A federal District Court in Alabama decided that certain portions of the 1965 Voting Rights Bill were unconstitutional. An appeal lay to the Supreme Court, which reversed the Alabama judge.

b When judgment has been given in a civil suit involving the anti-trust laws, the Federal Communications Act or the Interstate Commerce Act, the statutes themselves provide for a direct appeal to the Supreme Court, as long as the United States or one of its agents is a party to the action.

The anti-trust laws, in particular, encompass many more areas of our lives than most people might realize.[3]

Example

The Sherman Anti-trust Act applied to restraints imposed by the NCAA on televising college football games. When a university's Board of Trustees brought an action, the Supreme Court held that by imposing limits on televised games, the NCAA restricted the place of intercollegiate athletes in the national life.[4]

Example

You and your best friend buy up all the factories which make compact disc players. The Justice Department files a suit against you under the Sherman Anti-Trust Act and says you have established a monopoly. If you lose, you may appeal to the Supreme Court.

c When a three-judge court (which is required by some congressional Acts) gives an injunction (an order to do something or to stop doing something) in a suit to restrain enforcement of state or federal statutes or orders of some federal agencies.[5]

Example

A three-judge panel is required to hear questions arising from some aspects of the 1964 Civil Rights Act and to issue injunctions. If a panel orders a state to cease enforcement of a state statute requiring segregation in restaurants, an appeal by the state would lie to the Supreme Court.

FEDERAL CIRCUIT COURTS OF APPEALS

a When a federal law or treaty is held unconstitutional[6] as long as the United States or one of its employees is a party to the suit.

Example

If a Circuit Court of Appeals held the Medicare Amendment to the Social Security Act unconstitutional, an automatic appeal would lie to the Supreme Court.

b When a state statute is declared unconstitutional.[7]

Example

In a labor-management case, if a circuit court declared a state statute unconstitutional as in conflict with federal laws governing union elections, an appeal would lie to the Supreme Court.

STATE SUPREME COURTS[8]

a   When it has held unconstitutional a federal law or treaty.

Example

If the supreme court of a state declared a federal civil rights law unconstitutional, an appeal would lie directly to the Supreme Court.

b   When a state court has upheld a state law which is in necessary conflict with a federal law and therefore the federal law has been invalidated by implication.

Example

A state law requires children to go to school until they are 18. A boy, 17, is drafted into the Army. The state supreme court upholds his conviction as a juvenile delinquent, based on his truancy from school. An appeal would lie to the Supreme Court.

Those are the instances in which the Supreme Court *must* hear an appeal. They are somewhat rare. The majority of the Court's cases arise on what is know as "writs of certiorari." This means "to be informed." A person asks the court to hear his case and the Court issues a writ of certiorari to the lower court to "inform itself" about the case. The Court does not have to hear these cases and in fact only does so if it thinks a substantial question of law which is of national importance is presented.

Example

1   The Gideon case (see Amendment 6) was brought before the Supreme Court on a writ of certiorari. Gideon charged that he had been convicted of a crime in state court but denied the right to be furnished with an attorney. The court decided that this involved a question of national importance and agreed to hear his case.[9]

2   John Doe is in the state penitentiary awaiting execution for murder. If no substantially important legal question is presented in the record of his case, the Supreme Court will not consider it, regardless of the obvious importance of the matter to Doe.

These aspects of the jurisdiction of the federal courts are not in the Constitution. They are matters of practice, self-imposed regulations of the Supreme Court or established by Acts of Congress. However, all these regulations are established within the framework of constitutional provisions on the subject.

SECTION 1

The judicial Power of the United States, shall be vested in one supreme Court, and in such inferior Courts as the Congress may from time to time ordain and establish. The Judges, both of the supreme and inferior Courts, shall hold their Offices during good Behaviour, and shall, at stated Times, receive for their Services a Compensation, which shall not be diminished during their Continuance in Office.

We have already seen that judicial power is the power to decide an actual case. The courts will not hear a "political question," which is one properly decided by the executive or legislative branches.

Examples

1   The Supreme Court will not hear claims by two ambassadors both of whom claim to represent the same country. Recognition of foreign diplomats is determined by the President alone.[10]

2   The Supreme Court refused to intervene in the questions raised by the credentials committee's decisions to seat certain delegates to the 1972 Democratic convention on the ground that the matter was a "political" question and should be determined by the normal processes of the convention rules, not the judiciary.[11]

A person must have a genuine interest in a matter before the court before he may bring an action. For example, the Supreme Court held that a conservation club was unable to bring a suit against federal officials who were allowing commercial activities within a national game refuge, which the club believed to be illegal. The Court held that the club could not show that it or any of its members were damaged by the activities in any way other than that they disapproved of them. The Club, therefore, was held not to have the necessary interest to bring the suit unless it amended its complaint to allege injuries to individual members.[12]

Since Congress could starve a judge into resigning if they had the power to cut his salary if they disagreed with his decisions, this clause of the Constitution is designed to facilitate judicial independence.

SECTION 2

1 a The judicial Power shall extend to all Cases, in Law and Equity, arising under this Constitution, the Laws of the United States, and Treaties made, or which shall be made, under their Authority;

   b to all Cases affecting Ambassadors, other public Ministers and Consuls;

   c to all Cases of admiralty and maritime Jurisdiction;

   d to Controversies to which the United States shall be a Party;

   e to Controversies between two or more States;

   f between a State and Citizens of another State;

   g between Citizens of different States;

   h between Citizens of the same State claiming Lands under Grants of different States, and

   i between a State, or the Citizens thereof, and foreign States, Citizens or Subjects.

2 In all Cases affecting Ambassadors, other public Ministers and Consuls, and those in which a State shall be Party, the supreme Court shall have original Jurisdiction. In all the other Cases before mentioned, the supreme Court shall have appellate Jurisdiction, both as to Law and Fact, with such Exceptions, and under such Regulations as the Congress shall make.

3 The trial of all Crimes, except in Cases of Impeachment, shall be by Jury; and such Trial shall be held in the State where the said Crimes shall have been committed; but when not committed within any State, the Trial shall be at such Place or Places as the Congress may by Law have directed.

CLAUSE 1a A case arising under the Constitution and laws of the United States is one for which a correct decision depends upon the construction of either. It may be an appeal from a state supreme court.

Example

In the Gideon case, Gideon claimed that his rights under the amendments to the Federal Constitution had been abridged by state law. This, therefore arose "under the Constitution of the United States."[13]

b Ambassadors *from* foreign countries *to* the United States are tried or sued in federal courts. Our ambassadors *to* foreign countries are tried, when at home, in ordinary state courts unless another federal question is presented.

Example

The Ambassador from the Country of X to this country runs over and kills a child. He is prosecuted for manslaughter in federal court.

However, since ambassadors and other representatives of foreign countries may plead "diplomatic immunity" and legally remove themselves from the reach of our courts, few are successfully tried or sued.

c Admiralty and maritime jurisdiction confers the right to try all cases involving shipping in the federal courts.

Example

You are on a United States owned cruise ship. You fall over a rope which was left on the deck and break your leg. You sue the shipping company in federal court.

d   The United States may not be sued at all unless it consents, but in most cases it does.

Example

You are run down by a mail truck. You would sue for damages in federal court.

e   If one state sues another state, it is heard in federal court in order not to prejudice the cause of the state in whose courts the case would not be heard, not to benefit the state in whose courts the case would be tried.

Example

Pennsylvania and Ohio sued under the original jurisdiction of the Supreme Court to prevent West Virginia from forbidding producers of natural gas found there to pipe it out of the state.[14]

The Supreme Court usually decides to hear as part of its original jurisdiction suits brought by one state against another involving boundary disputes.[15] These are by no means matters resolved since the days of the Eighteenth and Nineteenth Century explorers and map-makers. Almost every year, the Court hears at least one boundary case.

f   The 11th Amendment has modified the clause about suits between a state and citizens of another state.

g   A suit between citizens of different states may be tried (but not necessarily) in federal court *if* the amount in controversy is at least $15,000. Congress imposed this limit in order to reduce the workload of the courts.

Example

You are involved in a collision with a driver from out of state. You sue him for $25,000. The suit may be tried in federal court but it may also be tried in state court.

The framers of the Constitution believed that this provision was necessary to secure the rights of the out-of-state citizen against local prejudice in state courts.

h   The clause about land grants is now obsolete.

i   The last clause has also been modified by the 11th Amendment.

CLAUSE 2   We have already seen what the power to hear an appeal (review) a case entails. The original jurisdiction of the Supreme Court means that in some cases it may hear a case from the beginning, and in this case it, of course, considers the facts as well as the law. Although the Court has the power to hear these cases in its original jurisdiction, it does not have to, and it may refuse a case of original jurisdiction if the state or ambassador can obtain an adequate hearing in a lower federal court.

Example

South Carolina brought a suit in 1965 to have the Voting Rights Act of 1965 declared unconstitutional. The Supreme Court heard the case in original jurisdiction and upheld the constitutionality of the law.[16]

Theoretically, Congress has the power under this clause to remove various sorts of cases from the jurisdiction of the Supreme Court. Whenever the Supreme Court hands down unpopular decisions, such as some of the ones striking down segregated school systems or the abortion cases, there are always harangues from outraged people to abolish that part of the Court's jurisdiction. Fortunately, however, Congress has never done this.

CLAUSE 3   This right is also guaranteed by the 6th Amendment.

SECTION 3

1   Treason against the United States, shall consist only in levying War against them, or in adhering to their Enemies, giving them Aid and Comfort. No Person shall be convicted of Treason unless on the Testimony of two Witnesses to the same overt Act, or on Confession in open Court.

2   The Congress shall have power to declare the Punishment of Treason, but no Attainder of Treason shall work Corruption of Blood, or Forfeiture except during the Life of the Person attainted.

CLAUSE 1 Since treason is the most serious crime known to the law, the framers of the Constitution wished to make absolutely certain that the innocent could not be convicted. A person who is in sympathy with the enemy but does not perform any act to aid them is not a traitor.

A person can only be tried for treason during a declared war. Persons accused of selling secrets or other acts of espionage during times of peace are tried for violating the espionage statutes, the national security laws or other federal statutes.

CLAUSE 2 This clause was inserted into the Constitution to prevent the effects on the traitor's family which were accepted by English law. "Attainder of treason" means that the traitor's estate is forfeited to the government. "Corruption of blood" means that the traitor's heirs would not inherit land from him, claim title to land they had already obtained from the traitor nor, in turn, will the land to their own descendants.

Article Four

THIS ARTICLE deals with relationships among the states, admission of new states to the Union, territorial governments and the responsibilities of the federal government to the states.

SECTION 1

Full Faith and Credit shall be given in each State to the public Acts, Records, and judicial Proceedings of every other State. And the Congress may by general Laws prescribe the Manner in which such Acts, Records and Proceedings shall be proved, and the Effect thereof.

This is known as the "full faith and credit" clause. All states must give recognition to the laws made and the judicial decrees rendered in other states.

Examples

1 Marriages legally contracted in one state are valid in all others.

2 A child legally adopted in one state is the legitimate child of his adoptive parents in all states.

3 A is sued by B for breach of contract. A has promised to sell his car to B and accepts B's money but refuses to deliver his car. B sues him and obtains a judgment for damages, but A flees to another state with the car and with B's money. Instead of being required to go after A and sue him again, B sends his judgment to a court where A is and they will make A pay.

This does not apply to professional licenses, which are neither statutes nor judicial decrees. A doctor or lawyer licensed to practice in one state is not automatically licensed in another. Furthermore, courts do not have to recognize decrees granted by the courts of foreign countries. However, this clause does require that federal courts recognize state laws and decrees.

Decrees in one state, to be recognized in another, must meet certain tests for entitlement to full faith and credit. For example, certain "quickie" divorces may not be valid in all states although certain specific circumstances must have occurred before a state may declare a divorce invalid.

Example

John Smart and his wife and Dora Darling and her husband all live in the same state. John and Dora decide that they prefer each other to their current spouses and leave home and go to a state where divorces are easily obtainable. They wait the required period and then file their divorce petitions, in which they state that they are residents of the divorcing state. They obtain their decrees, marry, and go to their original residence. Their divorces *may* be invalid and they *may* be guilty of bigamy.[1]

However, if a person is a legal resident of one state, his divorce must be upheld by all other states. A student away at school or a member of the Armed Forces may ordinarily file for divorce in his home state.

Child custody decrees sometimes may not be given full faith and credit if the party wishing to override the decree of another court can show that the best interests of the child would be served by a change of custody.[2]

SECTION 2

1 The Citizens of each State shall be entitled to all Privileges and Immunities of Citizens in the several States.

2 A Person charged in any State with Treason, Felony, or other Crime, who shall flee from Justice, and be found in another State, shall on Demand of the executive Authority of the State from which he fled, be delivered up, to be removed to the State having Jurisdiction of the Crime.

3 [No Person held to Service or Labour in one State, under the Laws thereof, escaping into another, shall, in Consequence of any Law or Regulation therein, be discharged from such Service or Labour, but shall be delivered up on Claim of the Party to whom such Service or Labour may be due.]

CLAUSE 1 A state may not discriminate against citizens of another state temporarily within its jurisdiction. All citizens of all states are entitled to protection by the government of any state in which they are physically present.[3]

Example

A state law which provided that the police would not answer calls from out of state citizens temporarily in their state would violate this section.

All citizens have the right to acquire property in any state.[4]

Example

A state law which stated that citizens of another state could not buy summer homes in that state would violate this clause.

Citizens of every state have the right to travel through all the other states.[5] The federal government, of course, controls the right of people in this country to travel abroad. While most people who are United States citizens may get passports without problems and go practically anywhere they wish, the government does have the right to forbid travel to some countries for foreign policy or safety reasons. For example, travel to Cuba has been banned for some time, and in 1984 the Supreme Court held that this was constitutional.[6] At the time of writing, United States passports may not be used to travel to a few countries the State Department considers too dangerous, such as Libya and Lebanon.

Citizens also have the right to writs of habeas corpus, and any state tax laws imposing higher taxes on nonresidents than on residents violate this clause. However, in matters relating to its own government, such as prescribing residency requirements for voter registration, a state may make reasonable rules.[7]

The Voting Rights Act,[8] however, provides that any person who is registered to vote in his home state and who moves to another state at least thirty days prior to a presidential election must be allowed to vote for president and vice-president even though they have not met residency requirements to vote for any other office. The voter in these circumstances may alternatively elect to vote absentee in his former home state. All states are now required by the same Act to permit absentee voting in presidential elections. This provision was upheld by the Supreme Court in *Oregon v. Mitchell*.[9]

State residency requirements for voting in state and local elections may not be longer than the minimum period which may be reasonably required to permit the voter to become knowledgeable about the candidates for office.[10] Fifty days, for example, has been upheld by the Supreme Court as reasonable.[11] Further, a state may still make reasonable, non-discriminatory restrictions on who may vote. Absentee ballots, for example, do not have to be provided to those detained in jail awaiting trial.[12]

CLAUSE 2 This clause permits, but does *not* require, a governor to extradite (return) a person who has fled a criminal charge or has been convicted of a crime in another state and has come into the governor's state. It is intended to provide a fast executive proceeding by which states can aid each other in preventing evasion of law.

Example

John Doe, convicted of murder, escapes from jail in South Carolina and is captured in Virginia. The South Carolina Governor requests the Governor of Virginia to keep Doe in custody until someone can get there to bring him back to South Carolina. Normally, the Governor of Virginia will oblige. However, if Doe can persuade him that he was unfairly convicted or denied due process of law, the Governor of Virginia may refuse to

extradite and there is nothing the Governor of South Carolina can do.

CLAUSE 3 This clause became obsolete when slavery was abolished.

SECTION 3

1 New States may be admitted by the Congress into this Union; but no new State shall be formed or erected within the Jurisdiction of any other State; nor any State be formed by the Junction of two or more States, or Parts of States, without the Consent of the Legislatures of the States concerned as well as of the Congress.

2 The Congress shall have Power to dispose of and make all needful Rules and Regulations respecting the Territory or other Property belonging to the United States; and nothing in this Constitution shall be so construed as to Prejudice any Claims of the United States, or of any particular State.

CLAUSE 1 The admission of new states into the Union is a legislative, not executive matter.
CLAUSE 2 Congress makes all laws, including

rules of criminal procedure, for all United States territories.

SECTION 4

The United States shall guarantee to every State in this Union a Republican Form of Government, and shall protect each of them against Invasion; and on Application of the Legislature, or of the Executive (when the Legislature cannot be convened) against domestic Violence.

A state bears the primary responsibility for establishing its own form of republican government, defined as a government by representatives chosen by the people.[13] If, however, a governor dissolved the legislature and had himself crowned emperor for life, the federal government would have the obligation to intervene. The federal government would also have the right to intervene against an elected government which devoted itself to sedition or violent overthrow of the federal government.[14]

The President may send federal troops or federalize and dispatch the National Guard to quell a domestic disturbance at the request of the governor.

This was a fairly common "strike-breaking" practice during the 1920's and 30's. The President's duty is to execute the laws passed by Congress and to enforce the decrees of the federal courts and to carry out his duty, he has full authority to dispatch troops into a state *without* the consent of and over the objections of the governor.

Example

Troops were dispatched to Little Rock, Arkansas and to the University of Mississippi to enforce the decrees of federal courts ordering integration of those schools.

Article Five

The Congress, whenever two-thirds of both Houses shall deem it necessary, shall propose Amendments to this Constitution, or, on the Application of the Legislatures of two-thirds of the several States, shall call a Convention for proposing Amendments, which, in either Case, shall be valid to all Intents and Purposes, as Part of this Constitution, when ratified by the Legislatures of three-fourths of the several States, or by Conventions in three-fourths thereof, as the one or the other Mode of Ratification may be proposed by the Congress: Provided that no Amendment which may be made prior to the Year One Thousand eight hundred and eight shall in any Manner affect the first and fourth Clauses in the Nineth Section of the first Article; and that no State, without its Consent, shall be deprived of its equal Suffrage in the Senate.

THIS ARTICLE deals with the procedures for amendment of the Constitution. It should be noted that the power to amend is strictly a legislative power. Unlike ordinary Acts of Congress which require the signature or veto of the President, the President has nothing to do with the amendment of the Constitution.[1] The proposed amendment, once adopted by Congress, is sent directly to the state legislatures.

An amendment has never been proposed by conventions called by the state legislatures. The usual method of amending the Constitution is that a proposal is made by two-thirds of a quorum in both houses of Congress and it is then sent to the state legislatures for ratification. When three-fourths of the legislatures have ratified it, it becomes part of the Constitution without further action.

Most proposed amendments incorporate a clause giving a time limit for ratification.

Article Six

1 All Debts contracted and Engagements entered into, before the Adoption of this Constitution, shall be as valid against the United States under this Constitution, as under the Confederation.

2 This Constitution, and the Laws of the United States which shall be made in Pursuance thereof; and all Treaties made, or which shall be made, under the Authority of the United States, shall be the supreme Law of the Land; and the Judges in every State shall be bound thereby, any Thing in the Constitution or Laws of any State to the Contrary notwithstanding.

3 The Senators and Representatives before mentioned, and the Members of the several State Legislatures, and all executive and judicial Officers, both of the United States and of the several States, shall be bound by Oath or Affirmation, to support this Constitution; but no religious Test shall ever be required as a Qualification to any Office or public Trust under the United States.

CLAUSE 1   This clause is now obsolete.

CLAUSE 2   The United States government has authority extending over the whole territory of the Union and its authority acts upon all the states and upon all the people of the states. As we have seen, the powers of the federal government are restricted by the Constitution, but as far as its powers extend, they are supreme. The Constitution, federal laws passed under it and the Supreme Court's interpretation of them are the supreme law of the land.

Any law of any state, so far as it conflicts with any valid law of the federal government, is null and void.

Example

An Act of Congress allows aliens with G-4 visas, those given to foreign nationals who are in this country because they are officers or employees of international organizations, to establish legal domiciles in this country. The University of Maryland refused to allow students with G-4 visas whose families lived in Maryland to qualify for in-state tuition and other benefits accorded all other students from Maryland. The Supreme Court held that this policy violated the Supremacy Clause.[1]

Decisions of the Supreme Court, where relevant, are binding on all state courts, even if they conflict with state laws. In short, the duty rests on *all* courts, state and federal, to guard, protect and enforce every right guaranteed by the United States Constitution.[2]

CLAUSE 3   All congressmen, all federal judges, the President, all governors, all state judges and all state legislators take oaths when they assume their offices that they will support the Constitution of the United States. This is the first duty they assume.[3]

When, notwithstanding the oaths they have taken, state officials fail to obey the commands of the Constitution, it is the duty of the federal courts to secure the rights of those to whom the officials have denied them.[4]

Example

If the governor of a state refuses to obey a federal court order to integrate a public school, he has not only disobeyed the law, which may result in his arrest for contempt of court, he has also disobeyed his oath, which he took freely and voluntarily, when he assumed his office.[5]

However, as is true of most major philosophical problems, there are two sides to this question. Some officials argue that obedience to this provision of the Constitution does not require them to submit when federal officials, particularly federal judges, extend federal authority beyond what has been historically considered to be the limits of federal power. This, it is felt, results in a violation of the oath to "uphold the Constitution" which the federal judge himself has taken.

Article VI of the Constitution remains, however, the foundation stone of our system of federal government.

Article Seven

The Ratification of the Conventions of nine States, shall be sufficient for the Establishment of this Constitution between the States so ratifying the Same. DONE in Convention by the Unanimous Consent of the States present the Seventeenth Day of September in the Year of our Lord one thousand seven hundred and Eighty seven and of the Independence of the United States of America the Twelfth. IN WITNESS whereof We have hereunto subscribed our Names.

THE FINAL ARTICLE of the Constitution provided for the original ratification by the states. March 4, 1789 was the day fixed for commencing operation of the new government under the Constitution, but because George Washington was late in arriving to assume his duties as President, the Articles of Confederation continued in effect until he was finally inaugurated on April 30, 1789.

The Bill of Rights

THE BILL OF RIGHTS consists of the first ten Amendments to the Constitution. Many citizens of the newly formed United States remembered too vividly for comfort the power of the King of England and urged their states not to ratify the Constitution until some provisions were made to limit the power of the central government against the rights of the individual citizen. The first ten Amendments, along with two more that were not ratified, were proposed to the legislatures of the states by the first Congress in September, 1789 and declared to be ratified in 1791.

Many of the provisions in the Bill of Rights concern the rights of a person accused of crime. When the Constitution and these Amendments were written, a conscious decision was made that where an individual's rights conflict with protection of society from criminal activity, the individual is more important. Our system of justice is predicated on the idea that it is better to let a guilty person go free than to convict an innocent one. A person charged with a crime is presumed to be innocent until he is convicted by a jury. It is not up to him to prove that he didn't do it. It is up to the government to prove that he did. The basic difference between a democracy and a totalitarian state is that in a democracy individuals are free of compulsion to agree with governmental actions that they think are wrong.

Because we are free to speak, write and vote as we please, changes in our government arise from the ballot box, not by revolution. A state in which the right to dissent is abridged is not a democratic state although it may be a benevolent dictatorship. From time to time well-meaning citizens wish to restrict the right of others to disagree with the government and claim that certain beliefs are "un-American."

The American nation was founded on a theory of respect for the dignity of all men and consequently for their views, however absurd or repugnant they may be. If we refuse to let a person with whom we disagree speak his mind (as long as he is not inciting a specific criminal act), we have, basically, denied the fundamental principles of democracy and substituted a totalitarian method of requiring obedience to the government. On paper, our Constitution contains rights that are in many cases quite similar to rights "guaranteed" to the Soviet people under their Constitution. The difference, therefore, between a democracy and a totalitarian state is a basic respect for the rights of all people and not just those with whom we happen to agree. There is an old saying that "a chain is only as strong as its weakest link" and this is never more true than in the relationship between government and citizens. When the rights of all people, no matter how annoying some of them may be to the majority, are not protected, and when the most ridiculous view is not protected as much as the most sensible, our system of law and our basic philosophy of human rights have broken down. If the government is empowered to pass a law today that makes it a crime to worship the sun, tomorrow it may well be a crime to be an orthodox Protestant. When infringements of fair play are accepted in some cases—denial of a fair trial to a "notorious criminal," in which case people may say "he got what he deserved," the next step may be transgressions of our basic principles against whomever the government chooses to persecute at the moment. Our legal system is not set up to guarantee rights to the "nice people." It is set up by this Constitution and these Amendments to protect the rights of *all* the people.

Amendment One

Congress shall make no law respecting an establishment of religion, or prohibiting the free exercise thereof, or abridging the freedom of speech, or
of the press, or the right of the people peaceably to assemble, and to petition the Government for a redress of grievances.

ALTHOUGH in early colonial times, some settlers had fled from Europe for *freedom to worship* as they pleased and then required the other members of their colonies to worship with them, as settlement progressed it was more important to have help with Indians, farming and other problems than it was to maintain religious conformity. By 1787 when the Constitution was written, the framers knew that it was necessary to build a wall between church and state. Tolerance was a matter of necessity. They did not intend the government to be opposed to either religious practice or to religion itself, but they meant to make it quite clear that religion is none of the government's business. This clause prohibits the federal government and, construed with the 14th Amendment, the state governments, from dictating what a person may believe about religion, what forms of religious exercise he may practice, or that he may believe in religion at all. The only restraint permitted any branch of the government is that it may prohibit religious practices that endanger the physical health of the citizens. It may not restrict any religious or antireligious belief, however unorthodox it may be.[1]

Examples

1   A child may not be required to salute the flag at school if this violates the religious beliefs of his parents. The community health and safety are not threatened by a refusal to salute the flag.

2   A religious group that handles dangerous snakes as part of its worship may be ordered to cease the practice. This is a justifiable prohibition to protect the health of the community of which the church members are a part.

3   While the draft was in effect, Congress provided exemptions from combat duty in Viet Nam for conscientious objectors whose religious beliefs precluded them from engaging in war. However,

those young men who wished to be granted conscientious objector status were required to submit to draft regulations and to be inducted into the service. After entering, they were placed in clerical or hospital jobs. Failure to obey draft laws was thought to endanger the safety of the country and therefore, an individual's religious beliefs were required to give way to the national interest.

4   A court may order a blood transfusion given to a seriously ill child over the religious objections of the child's parents. The courts have held that a parent's religious freedom does not extend to letting a child die when reasonable medical care would save it. Here, the health of the child is more important to the community than the parent's right to a particular belief.[2]

In all cases where restrictions on religious practices have been held constitutional, there was a clear and immediate danger to some vital aspect of the community's life.[3]

Children whose Amish parents objected, for religious reasons, to education beyond the eighth grade were held by the Supreme Court to have a valid exemption from state compulsory education laws. The Court held that a high school education was not so vital to a child's well-being that the state could require it over parental objections based on religion.[4]

Although conscientious objector status is conferred by Congress and is not a constitutional right, numerous decisions interpreting the conscientious objector section of the Selective Service Act[5] arose during the Viet Nam war. The Supreme Court held that an objector had a valid claim to that status even though his objection is not based on religion. In *Welsh v. United States*[6] the Supreme Court decided that a registrant who objected to participation in the Armed Forces for reasons based on nontheistic philosophical, sociological, and historical grounds could not be denied exemption as a conscientious objector. To so limit the right to those who are motivated by religious reasons, the Court said, would violate the nonbeliever's freedom from religion.

Conscientious objector status is, however, only granted to those who object to all wars, not just the one currently in question. In *Gillette v. United States* and *Negre v. Larsen*,[7] the Court considered the cases of two draft-eligible men who stated that they had no moral objection to participation in a war in defense of the United States. They objected, however, to participation in the Viet Nam conflict for both religious and political reasons. The Court held that the conscientious objector section of the Selective Service Act exempted only those persons who refused to participate in any war, not those who were opposed to participation on a selective basis, even if their objection to the particular war was based on religion.

Since the 14th Amendment makes the right of freedom of and from religion applicable to the state governments, no state may engage in any activity that infringes upon a citizen's right to believe or disbelieve as he chooses. The famous "School Prayer" cases have held that a public school may not require a student to participate in any religious observances. Private schools may, of course, teach any religious beliefs they wish.

Examples

1   A teacher paid by the Ministerial Association in a community came into the public school classroom and taught religious education classes. Although children whose parents did not wish them to participate could be excused, the Supreme Court held that such instruction in a public building was lending the force of the state and the school to the beliefs of the teacher and to permit such instruction violated the First Amendment.[8]

2   In another case, public school children were released early and reported to various churches where classes in religious education were held. Students who did not participate remained at school and had study halls. The courts held that since no public facility was being used to promote religion, the practice, known as "released time" was perfectly constitutional.[9]

3   A state legislature passed a law requiring Bible reading in each home room each morning. The Supreme Court held that this required a religious practice and that such compulsory religion violated the principles of the 1st Amendment.[10]

4   The New York Board of Regents wrote a non-denominational prayer and required its use in public schools. The Supreme Court held that a branch of government that writes and requires a prayer has established a religion and that this, therefore, was unconstitutional.[11]

5   A state statute required one minute of silent prayers or meditation each day in all the state's public schools. The Supreme Court held the statute unconstitutional because its only stated purpose was to return prayer to the schools.[12]

6   Public high school students established a "spiritual growth club." The School Board denied them the right to have prayer meetings at school and the students sued. The Supreme Court held in 1986 that the Establishment Clause prevailed and upheld the School Board.[13]

The theory behind these decisions was that the matter of religious education is a matter for the home, not the school. The Court took the view that a parent whose child is in public school should not have his child taught something about religion in which the parent does not believe and does not wish the child to believe. It is perfectly acceptable to teach the Bible from a literary instead of a theological viewpoint, since knowledge of its contents is important to a well-rounded education, but the line is drawn at the point where any conversion of a student could result.[14]

Statutes that prohibited teaching about evolution in public schools were found unconstitutional as a violation of the right of freedom of religion in *Epperson v. Arkansas*.[15] The court held that such statutes favored the religious view of creation over those held by persons who believed in evolution, thus constituting an establishment of religion by the state.

Cadets at the United States service academies may not be required to attend church or compulsory chapel services.[16] The Armed Forces may, however, restrict some aspects of religious freedom among military personnel. For example, the Supreme Court held that it was not a violation of his right of religious freedom for the Air Force to refuse to let an officer who was an Orthodox Jew wear his yarmulke indoors while he was required to be in uniform.[17] Uniform regulations forbid any headwear indoors.

The government supports religion in any number of perfectly constitutional ways.[18] For example, a city government decided to have a Nativity scene on the public green at Christmas time and the Supreme Court held that it did not infringe on the rights of religious freedom for those in the community who are not Christians.[19] Chaplains in the Armed Forces are commissioned officers and are paid by the government. State legislatures and Congress have chaplains.[20] Prison chaplains are also paid by the states. To eliminate chaplains would constitute "prohibiting the free exercise of religion." An ordinary citizen is free to go to church or to stay home, as he chooses. This is not true of a serviceman or of a prisoner. If a person is in jail or on patrol in the jungle, the church must come to him if he is to worship.

A prisoner has the right of freedom of religion during incarceration. If he belongs to a sect for which no chaplain or facility is provided by prison authorities, he must be allowed the same opportunities to exercise his religious beliefs as is given to those prisoners who belong to more conventional religious bodies already recognized by prison officials.[21]

Tax exemptions are granted to churches as well as to nonreligious charitable organizations such as colleges and hospitals. The question of tax exemptions for church-owned property was upheld by the Supreme Court in 1970.[22] Questions of tax exemptions for property owned by churches, hospitals, and universities usually do not involve issues about levying taxes on the church or classroom buildings themselves, but rather on income-producing property owned by the church or other organization.

Example

The Faithful Church receives ownership of a girdle factory by the will of its former owner, Mr. Snap. The church does not pay either income or property taxes on either the factory or the profits that it derives from the sale of its girdles. Across the street from the church's Hold Tight factory, there is a Skinny Look girdle factory owned by Mr. Pop, who has to pay all the usual taxes on his factory and his sales. The church's girdles can, therefore, be sold at a lower price than Mr. Pop's girdles. The question involved in these cases is, therefore, the fairness of this exemption to other taxpayers, particularly to competitors in the same business.

It is, however, clear that the workers in profit-making businesses owned by religious organizations must receive minimum wages, overtime pay and all other employment benefits that accrue to workers employed by any other corporation.[23]

State aid to parochial education has been the subject of many Supreme Court decisions. In 1947, the Supreme Court held in *Everson v. Board of Education*[24] that allowing parochial school children to ride buses owned by the public school system did not violate the doctrine of church and state because the assistance was to the children, not to the school. The same conclusion was reached in *Board of Education v. Allen*[25] when the court held that school districts could furnish books dealing with secular subjects to

parochial schools. The children, not the schools, were again held to be the beneficiaries of the programs.

In 1971, the Supreme Court developed a three-part test to determine if state action relating to religious schools is constitutional. If the state action (1) has a primary secular purpose, (2) does not have the principal effect of either advancing or inhibiting religion and (3) does not create excessive governmental entanglement with religion, it is constitutional.[26] In applying these guidelines, the Supreme Court has refused to allow state aid to parochial schools in the form of state maintenance and repair grants[27] or tuition reimbursement.[28] It is also unconstitutional for public school teachers to spend parts of their days teaching at parochial schools even if they provide remedial education otherwise unavailable in the parochial school.[29] The Supreme Court has felt that all of these activities created a symbolic link between government and religion and directly promoted religion. On the other hand, the Court ruled in 1983 that a state statute allowing deduction from state tax returns of private school tuition did not entangle the state in religion because the deduction applied to all private schools, not just those affiliated with religious groups.[30]

The test is more easily satisfied in cases involving higher education. The Higher Education Facilities Act of 1963[31] that provided federal construction grants for secular-use facilities in church-related colleges was held constitutional in *Tilton v. Richardson*.[32] The Court reasoned that there was less likely to be religious involvement in secular subjects at the college level than in elementary and secondary schools. Furthermore, the college grants were for construction, not continuing aid to the colleges' programs and operating budgets. Grants to college students are also permissible even if the student is attending a church-related college. For example, state aid to a blind college undergraduate studying for the ministry at a church-related college did not violate provisions against the establishment of religion because aid to blind students was available regardless of where they enrolled or what they studied.[33]

In essence, unless religious activities are dangerous to the health of the community, no part of the state or federal government may stop anyone from practicing his religion, or from believing whatever he wishes, and it may not make him go to church at all. State universities, for example, may not constitutionally ban worship on their campuses any more than they may require it.[34] However, if a person is under the control of the government in some way, the government must assure him or her the right to worship if he or she chooses.

Freedom of speech means that we have a right to advocate ideas. This guarantee is not confined to an expression of ideas that are conventional or shared by the majority. Freedom of speech and of the press permit us to exchange ideas for bringing about political and social changes desired by the people and to keep the people fully informed about the acts or misconduct of public officials. All ideas must be protected, no matter how unpopular they may be. An unorthodox or controversial idea is entitled to as much protection as any other, unless it conflicts directly and immediately with vital national interests.[35] All persons living under our legal system have the right to hold, express, teach or advocate any opinion, and to join with others to express it, although the opinion may be repugnant to the vast majority of the citizens.

As was true of the freedom of religious practice, however, this right is not an absolute right. The amendment does not give anyone the right to speak or write in a way that injures another person or his property, that corrupts public morals, that incites criminal activity, or that advocates a specific action for overthrowing the government by force.[36]

As we saw, under Article I, a Member of Congress cannot be sued for slander for anything he or she says on the floor of Congress. All other persons who defame another person may be sued and damages may be recovered from them. There is not, for example, any immunity from defamation because it is expressed in a petition to the government. If, for example, a person is nominated for a governmental position and another person writes defamatory letters to the appointing official, with the result that the nomination is withdrawn, he or she may recover damages from the writer of the letters.[37] If the person defamed is a public official, the Supreme Court has held that criticism of public officials is so vital to the prevention of tyranny that the official must show that the defamation was made with knowledge of its falsity and actuated by deliberate malice.[38] In any defamation suit, the burden of proof that the speech or writing was defamatory is almost always on the person who is suing for damages.[39]

Examples

1 Mrs. Doe tells Mrs. Roe that her next door neighbor, Mrs. Jones, is a crook. Mrs. Jones may recover damages from Mrs. Doe for slander unless Mrs. Doe can prove what she said is true.

2 Mrs. Doe makes a speech in which she says that Richard Roe, the governor of her state, is stupid and a crook. Before Roe may collect damages, he must prove (1) that Mrs. Doe was acting for malicious reasons, (2) that he is neither stupid nor a crook, and (3) that Mrs. Doe knew that he was smart and honest at the time she made her speech.

The Supreme Court has decided several cases under the "public official" doctrine. In one the court decided that for this purpose, a candidate for public office was a "public official." He, therefore, must prove actual malice.[40] Actual malice is considered to be a knowing disregard of the truth and not just an honest mistake of fact.

Examples

1 A magazine carried an article indicating that a policeman had been charged with brutality in criminal court. In fact, the policeman had been sued for damages in a civil case. The Supreme Court held that this error did not constitute "actual malice."[41]

2 The mayor of a city was alleged in a newspaper story to have been charged with perjury. The person actually charged was his brother. The Court held that no actual malice existed.[42]

Although a person may express any political theory he wishes, speech or writing that incites others to acts of violence is not protected by the Constitution if it is likely that violence will result.[43] Speech of this type is known as "seditious speech" if the desired result is violence against the government. However, the advocated act must be specific and immediate in order to constitute sedition.[44]

Examples

1 Henry Hoe stands on the street corner and makes a speech objecting to our government's policy in Latin America. He says that the President is a nitwit. This is permissible, because freedom of speech is designed to protect anyone's right to criticize the actions of the government.

2 Joe also stands on the corner and also makes a speech protesting the government's activities in Latin America. He says that the way to end the problem is to shoot everyone who works for the National Security Council. This speech is also not seditious because Joe has not advocated any immediate and specific act of violence.

3 In the example above, Joe continues by saying that he has guns and ammunition at his house on the corner and that his listeners must come with him, get the guns, and be off on his bus to Washington. He says that they will be on their way in half an hour to kill everyone who works

for the National Security Council. Joe may be arrested for sedition.

In order for speech to be restricted in the national interest, there must be a "clear and present danger" to an interest the government must protect, such as defense of the country, and it must be shown that the speech would have incited direct and illegal action.

A landmark case involving freedom of speech was decided on June 30, 1971. In *The New York Times v. United States* and *United States v. The Washington Post Co.*,[45] both papers had printed the classified Pentagon Papers, involving the government's activities in Viet Nam. These Papers had been leaked to them. The government sought to enjoin further publication. The Supreme Court held that the government could not enjoin material not yet published.

A student in a public school also has a right to freedom of speech and expression. He may not be punished for wearing symbols protesting governmental action or other noninflammatory, nonobscene expressions of opinion.[46] Schools may, however, prohibit behavior or expression of opinion, even if legal for an adult, that would interfere with other students' work or cause disorder. It is, for example, permissible to suspend a high school student who makes a sexually suggestive but nonobscene speech in assembly.[47] There are, however, limitations on the school's right to restrict free speech and free press rights of public school students. A school board, for example, does not have unlimited discretion to remove books from school libraries because new members of the board decide that they do not like the ideas expressed in those books.[48] College newspapers, with very few exceptions, have all of the First Amendment rights guaranteed to other newspapers.[49]

Freedom of the press, however, does not include immunity from legal investigation. A newspaper reporter does not have a right to refuse to answer grand jury questions concerning the identity of the reporter's informants. Even if the reporter was given the information in confidence, the Supreme Court has ruled that such information must be revealed if it is linked to the commission of a criminal act.[50]

Considered along with freedom of speech is the problem of what actions, when accompanied by speech, are protected under the First Amendment. What actions are, in the Supreme Court's words, "symbolic speech"? Several Supreme Court cases dealt with activities at meetings held to protest the war in Viet Nam. For example, the Court held that the federal statute that prohibited burning draft cards was constitutional.[51] A regulation which banned sleeping in Lafayette Park, which is across the street from the White House, was also upheld when people wished to camp there to protest the plight of the homeless. The Court held that sleep is not symbolic speech.[52] By contrast, the Supreme Court held that hanging the American flag upside down with a peace symbol attached to it was a protected form of expression.[53] Other antiwar protestors who turned in (instead of burning) their draft cards could not be punished by accelerated induction into the Armed Forces[54] or denied their student deferments.[55]

The 1st Amendment also involves books, newspapers, television, and radio programs. Obscene speech or writing is not protected by the First Amendment.[56] However, the problem is the definition of obscenity. The Supreme Court decided that it must be the final arbiter of obscenity and judge each book on its own merits.[57]

At one time, the Court's definition of obscenity required the presence of three elements: (1) the dominant theme must appeal to a prurient interest in sex; (2) it must affront contemporary community standards; and (3) it must be utterly without redeeming social value.[58] Since 1973 the Court has defined[59] obscenity as something that (1) appeals to prurient interests; (2) portrays, in a patently offensive way, sexual conduct specifically defined by an applicable state statute; and (3) taken as a whole, does not have serious literary, artistic, political, or social value. The standards to be applied are those of "the average person applying the contemporary community standard." Statutes forbidding importation of obscene material, even for private use,[60] sending obscene material through the mail,[61] and selling it knowing it to be obscene[62] have all been held to be constitutional.

Statutes that differentiate between what may be sold to minors as opposed to adults and that create a criminal offense of selling obscene material to minors have also been upheld.[63] However, an adult's possession of obscene material for his or her own use cannot be made a criminal offense.[64] This right of privacy, however, does not extend to the right of an adult to view obscene films in public theaters.[65] Ordinances, for example, that ban adult movie theaters within a certain distance of churches, schools, or homes are constitutional.[66] Statutes allowing criminal prosecution of persons selling films showing children engaging in sexual activities also do not violate the First Amendment.[67]

The only reason a book may be removed from a

store is that it is either seditious or obscene. Obscenity has been defined only in sexual terms and does not include the most graphic descriptions, in print or in a film, of physical violence, blood, gore, or pain. If a book is sacrilegious or otherwise offensive, it remains protected by the First Amendment.

Radio and television broadcasting fall into a different category. There is a basic right to read a book, but there is no right to broadcast.[68] Licenses for radio and television stations are issued by the Federal Communications Commission and may be revoked if the station is not broadcasting "in the public interest," which is much more restrictive than merely prohibiting seditious or obscene material. If a radio station broadcasts a number of bogus news bulletins, for example, its license could be revoked.

The Supreme Court protects advertising as "commercial speech."[69] Although it may be regulated, advertising by professionals is now permitted. State statutes that defined advertising by pharmacists[70] and attorneys[71] as "unprofessional conduct" were found by the Supreme Court to be unconstitutional.

The clause of the First Amendment pertaining to *peaceable assembly* protects the right to picket, a right that has been exercised in political, labor-management, and civil rights disputes.[72] Anti-foreign-policy demonstrators, for example, cannot be convicted of disorderly conduct simply because onlookers disagree with them.[73] A civilian has the similar right to distribute leaflets peacefully protesting United States foreign policy on a public street inside an open military base.[74]

A Chicago ordinance prohibited peaceful picketing for any reason other than a labor dispute within a certain distance of a school. The Supreme Court held that differentiating between peaceful picketing based on the substance of the picket violated the Equal Protection clause of the Fourteenth Amendment.[75] An ordinance prohibiting noise from pickets so close to a school that a disruption occurred was, however, constitutional.[76]

During the civil rights demonstrations of the 1960's, many cities required parade permits before a demonstration could be "legal." They then used the ordinances to prohibit demonstrations of which city officials disapproved. The Supreme Court, however, held that such ordinances were unconstitutional and that protesters were free to ignore them.[77] Reasonable traffic restrictions may, however, be enforced against demonstrators.[78]

In general, picketing is protected when it is for a lawful purpose—to publicize a grievance—and is conducted in an orderly manner. Disorder or violence by pickets, however, does not have to be tolerated.[79] If a hostile crowd gathers and the pickets are orderly, the police have a constitutional obligation to protect the picketers and ordering them to disperse because of their unpopular views is an infringement of their rights.[80] The First Amendment does not exist only for the expression of popular views.

A privately-owned shopping center has the right to bar political leaflets that have no relation to business conducted there.[81] However, where the leaflets concern matters involving any of the businesses within it, distribution cannot be prohibited.[82]

In short, there is a national commitment to the idea that debates on public issues must be uninhibited and our right to criticize cannot be denied. A government in a democracy must accept the fact that discussions of its policies are not always complimentary.

The right of *freedom of association* gives one the right to belong to any group he chooses and assures the citizen that he has the right to belong to any organization that agrees with him.[83]

A public college cannot, for example, refuse to recognize a student organization because the administration disagrees with its philosophy.[84] Only groups that are genuinely disruptive to activities of other students may be prohibited. A college newspaper may not be subject to censorship that cannot be applied to other newspapers.[85]

Federal statutes restricting the amounts of money Political Action Committees could contribute to the campaigns of presidential candidates who had accepted federal funds were held to violate the Committees' freedoms of speech and association.[86]

The right of association does not require the Attorney General to issue an entrance visa to an alien who has been invited to come to this country to lecture. The Attorney General may exclude any alien he considers "undesirable" and this authority is not restricted by the First Amendment rights of those who wish to hear the alien speak.[87] The Immigration and Naturalization Services may restrict aliens in this country in other ways as well. If an illegal alien who claims political refugee status wishes to avoid deportation, he or she must establish that there is a clear probability of political persecution if he or she goes home, not just that some people are being persecuted in his or her native country.[88] Also, an alien facing deportation may not object to the use of illegally obtained evidence if it is used against him or her in the deportation proceedings. The Supreme Court has ruled that the exclusionary rule (See Amendment Four) only involves rights in a criminal proceeding and deportation hearings are civil, not criminal.[89]

Freedom of association may also impose an obligation to associate. For example, many states require all lawyers who wish to practice there to belong to the state Bar Association in order to maintain professional standards. As long as dues are not used for political purposes, this is constitutionally permissible.

The *right of petition* is exemplified by the Declaration of Independence, a statement to the world explaining our rebellion against King George III. Petitions, marches and appeals to the state, local or national authorities are protected by this amendment and petitioners may not be arrested simply because the governmental official disagrees with them.

Amendment Two

A well regulated Militia, being necessary to the security of a free State, the right of the people to keep and bear Arms, shall not be infringed.

THIS AMENDMENT is not applicable to the states, which are free to regulate use and sale of firearms as they see fit.

One part of the "common law" or basic legal system that we inherited from England was the right to self-protection, which implies the right to own and bear arms. However, this right is not guaranteed to all citizens by the Constitution and if Congress chose to do so, it could place heavy restrictions on interstate sale of weapons. The purpose of this amendment is to provide for the effectiveness of the militia, which would presumably protect the citizen against unconstitutional usurpation of power by the federal government.[1] This amendment alone does not give all citizens the right to own weapons to use for duck-hunting if Congress wishes to restrict that right. It merely prevents the federal government from disarming the members of the National Guard.

Example

A man was convicted of possessing an unregistered machine gun. He contended that he was subject to enrollment in the State Militia (the National Guard) and that therefore he had a fundamental right under the Second Amendment to possess the gun. The Court held that the Second Amendment guarantees a collective, rather than an individual right to bear arms, which does not give any individual a personal right to own a machine gun.[2]

The 1968 Crime Control Act[3] provides that transportation of firearms in interstate commerce without compliance with certain regulations applicable to gun dealers only is a criminal offense. Transportation of weapons for sale without such a license which only dealers may obtain is a crime. The Supreme Court held in *United States v. Bass*[4] that the statute would be construed to mean that one violates the act only if the firearm was moving in interstate commerce or was on an interstate carrier such as an airplane, at the time it was discovered. Possession of a weapon which had been illegally brought into a state prior to the time it is discovered is not a violation of the act. Prosecution both for receiving an unlicensed firearm from interstate commerce and for possession of the firearm is considered double jeopardy, but either offense alone may be prosecuted.[5]

The 1968 Gun Control Act[6] provided that those businesses which had federal licenses to obtain firearms in interstate commerce for resale could be inspected by federal agents for violations of the law. The Supreme Court held in *United States v. Biswell*[7] that no warrant was necessary for an agent to inspect a gun dealer's premises.

Mandatory sentences for possession of a firearm during commission of a felony do not violate due process rights, the right to a jury trial, or any rights under this Amendment.[8]

Amendment Three

No Soldier shall, in time of peace be quartered in any house, without the consent of the Owner, nor in time of war, but in a manner to be prescribed by law.

THIS AMENDMENT has never been the subject of construction by the courts and has been unimportant since its adoption.

Amendment Four

The right of the people to be secure in their persons, houses, papers and effects, against unreasonable searches and seizures, shall not be violated, and no Warrants shall issue, but upon probable cause, supported by Oath or affirmation and particularly describing the place to be searched, and the persons or things to be seized.

No MATTER how important society's right to be protected from criminal behavior may be, the means used to restrict criminal activity must be lawful and constitutional. No one, no matter how obnoxious or dangerous, may be "railroaded" to jail without protection of his basic rights.

The right to go to our homes and be let alone by the government is a very precious freedom.

The rights of privacy and personal security protected by this amendment are regarded as essential to liberty.[1] Protection of one's privacy and possessions must be extended to all by both the states and the federal government.[2]

Usually, no one may be arrested without a warrant, an order signed by a judicial officer to arrest a named individual for a specified crime. A warrant may issue if a reasonable person would believe that the crime has, in fact, been committed and that the individual to be arrested has been involved in its commission.[3] In two situations, however, an arrest may take place without a warrant. In case of a serious crime, known as a felony, if there is no time to obtain a warrant, a policeman may arrest someone if he believes that a crime has been committed and that the person is involved. Shortly after such an arrest, a judge must determine that there is probable cause to continue to hold the person arrested.[4]

Examples

1   Officer Smith, a policeman, is walking past Mrs. Jones's store when she rushes out screaming "Help! Police!" She tells him that she has been robbed by a bandit who had a gun and took her cash register with him. She describes the man. Smith looks up and sees a man answering that description running and carrying a cash register. He may arrest the man.

2   In the same example, Smith does not see anyone, so he takes Mrs. Jones to the police station where she identifies the robber from a picture. A warrant is necessary before Smith may go to the man's house and arrest him.

An arrest without a warrant may also be made in the case of a minor infraction of criminal law, known as a misdemeanor, but usually only if the offense is committed in the presence of the arresting policeman. If the policeman is told about a misdemeanor and goes to the person's house without a warrant to arrest him, the arrest is invalid.[5]

Examples

1   Throwing paper on the street is usually a misdemeanor in most cities. If Officer Smith sees Dan Dumb throw a candy bar wrapper on the sidewalk, he may make an arrest.

2   If Ned Nasty comes up to Officer Smith and tells him that he saw Dan throw the candy wrapper on the sidewalk around the corner, Officer Smith may not arrest Dan without a warrant.

If a policeman without a warrant stops someone on the street to check his identity, it is not an "arrest" and is permissible if the reason for the inquiry is that the person looks like a picture on a wanted poster.[6] A state statute requiring all persons to identify themselves and account for their presence at the scene if asked to do so by a policeman, was so vague as to be unconstitutional.[7]

This Amendment prohibits police use of deadly force in the course of arresting someone unless the person poses a threat of death or serious injury to the policemen or others. For example, a man was escaping from a burglary when the officers arrived. He did not appear to be armed. A policeman shot and killed him. His father sued and the Supreme Court upheld the award of damages the jury had given.[8]

If a person is lawfully arrested, he may be searched at the police station and any evidence found may be used against him even if it is unrelated to the crime for which he was arrested.[9]

Example

Fred Foolish is arrested for being drunk and disorderly. When he is taken to the police station, he is searched and narcotics are found in his pocket. He may be arrested for possession of narcotics.

Only reasonable searches are allowed. For example, police officers may not hold a suspect down and pump out his stomach if they believe that he swallowed narcotics.[10]

The Supreme Court held that when a suspect is subject to valid arrest, although his person and the area immediately around him (such as the room in which he was found) may be searched, his entire house may not be searched unless the police have a search warrant as well as an arrest warrant.[11] If a person is arrested in the yard of his home, it is unconstitutional to go into the house without a search warrant.[12]

Example

Fred Felon is suspected of bank robbery. The police go to his house with an arrest warrant. He is sitting on the sofa in his living room watching television. After they have arrested him, the officers may search Fred and the area in which he is sitting. If they find loot from the robbery underneath the sofa cushions, it may be used in evidence. Unless they have a search warrant, they may not go upstairs and look in the bedroom closets.

Fingerprinting is constitutionally permissible only if it is undertaken pursuant to an arrest warrant based on reasonable cause to believe that the person whom the police wish to fingerprint has had something to do with the crime.[13]

Example

A suspect was arrested without probable cause and taken to the police station and fingerprinted. The fingerprints matched those found at the scene of a rape. The Supreme Court held that the fingerprints were not admissible as evidence because use of them violated the man's rights under the Fourth Amendment.[14]

Wholesale "dragnet arrests" and fingerprinting of large numbers of people in the hopes that at least one of them might subsequently be proved to have had something to do with the crime are not permitted, since it violates this amendment and the due process clause of the 14th Amendment.[15]

At the time of a lawful arrest, and in some other circumstances, a vehicle may be searched without a warrant if the searchers believe that it might contain evidence of a crime.[16] Obviously, if the searchers had to leave the car in order to go get a warrant, the car would not be there when they got back. For example, if a policeman stops a car for a traffic violation and a balloon floating freely within the car contains white powder that the policeman can see, the balloon may be seized and the car searched without a warrant.[17] A policeman may enter a car he has stopped for a traffic violation in order to check its registration. If, in the course of looking for the registration, he sees a gun, narcotics or other contraband, arrest of the driver and a search of the car are permitted.[18] A motor home is a "vehicle" if it is on a road or if it is capable of being driven. Therefore, it is permissible to search, without a warrant, a motor home that is parked and in which someone is living.[19]

Example

A roadblock is set up to capture an escaped criminal. Each car arriving at the barricade is examined. No warrant is required for these searches, and if illicit drugs are found where they can be seen by anyone opening the doors or trunk, the driver may be arrested.

After occupants of a car are arrested and the car has been removed to a police station, it may be searched without a warrant.[20] When the car is parked in front of a suspect's home or is otherwise not in use, however, a search warrant is usually required.[21] Before a warrantless search of a car, boat, plane, motor home, or other vehicle may be constitutionally conducted, the police must show that someone had the means to move it.

Any search except of an arrested person or of a vehicle must be conducted under a search warrant. A valid warrant must specify the location to be searched, the crime involved, and the evidence that the police believe they will find. If, however, either the arrest or the search has been conducted unconstitutionally, the evidence cannot be used against the accused.[22] A search must have been legal from the outset and valuable evidence found in the course of an unconstitutional search is still inadmissible in court.

Example

A woman killed her husband and tried to kill herself. She became frightened after she had swallowed what she believed to be a lethal dose of sleeping pills and called her daughter for help. The daughter called the police, who rushed to the home and found the woman unconscious and her husband's dead body. The women was sent to the hospital and one-half hour later, detectives searched her house without a warrant. Based on such things as letters they found, she was charged with second-degree murder. The Supreme Court held that the warrantless search violated her rights and the evidence was inadmissible.[23]

Restrictions on searches without warrants apply to law enforcement officers and situations that may lead to criminal proceedings. There may be other situations in which other persons, such as teachers, are entitled to conduct noncriminal searches without need for a warrant.

Example

A teacher discovered a 14-year-old girl smoking in the school bathroom. The student was sent to the Principal's office, where she denied that she had been smoking. The Assistant Principal opened her purse and found cigarettes, marihuana, and letters indicating that she was a drug dealer. She was reported to the juvenile authorities and the Supreme Court held that the search was legal.[24]

Similarly, a case worker's home visit to a family on public assistance is not considered to be a "search" and no warrant is necessary. A state statute providing that benefits may be terminated if the welfare recipient refuses to allow the social worker into the house is constitutional as long as the visit is made within reasonable hours and contains no elements of harassment.[25]

Searches of a defendant's body, such as removal of a bullet, present Fourth Amendment questions as well. While these may be permissible if there is no risk to the arrestee,[26] the state may not compel major surgery—one which requires general anesthesia, for example—to remove a bullet to be used in evidence.[27]

A legal search, with or without a warrant, may result in discovery of evidence of an unrelated crime. The Supreme Court has upheld seizure of the evidence as long as it was in plain view during the legal search.[28] The discovery must be genuinely accidental, however. When police lawfully enter a home (for example, when a resident consents to their coming in) and evidence of a crime is in plain view, they do not need a warrant to seize it.

Example

A college policeman observed a student walking on campus with an open bottle of gin. The student appeared to be younger than the legal age for drinking, so the policeman asked the student for his ID. The student said that he had left it in his dorm room and the policeman went with him to get it. When the student opened the door to his room, the policeman, standing out in the hall, saw marihuana and a pipe on top of a desk. When asked, the student's roommate, who was already in the room, handed over a quantity of marihuana. All of the drugs were seized and the seizure was upheld.[29]

No warrant is necessary for the police to look for something outside of a building or a private yard. For example, no warrant is necessary if the police fly over an open field,[30] observe marihuana growing there, and come back later and seize the plants.[31] There is no right of privacy outside except in the yard of a home. Even within a private yard, moreover, police may seize and use as evidence objects in plain view.[32]

A "plain view" search cannot be used as an excuse to find something the police suspect is on the premises but for which they have insufficient evidence to obtain a search warrant.[33]

Examples

1 A proper search warrant is obtained to search Joe Dumb's house for narcotics. While looking in a drawer in the kitchen, a reasonable place for narcotics to be hidden, the police find stolen jewelry. They may seize the jewelry and use it in evidence against Joe.

2 The police have a warrant to look in Joe's garage for a stolen car. The car is not there, but they look in a tool box and find the jewelry. Since the car could not have been hidden in the tool box, the jewelry may not be used in evidence against Joe.

Amendment Five

No person shall be held to answer for a capital, or otherwise infamous crime, unless on a presentment or indictment of a Grand Jury, except in cases arising in the land or naval forces, or in the Militia, when in actual service in time of War or public danger; nor shall any person be subject for the same offence to be twice put in jeopardy of life or limb; nor shall be compelled in any criminal case to be a witness against himself; nor be deprived of life, liberty, or property, without due process of law; nor shall private property be taken for public use, without just compensation.

THE FIFTH AMENDMENT guarantees the right to indictment by a grand jury in federal criminal cases, prohibits double jeopardy, protects against compulsory self-incrimination, guarantees due process of law in the federal courts and establishes the requirement that the government pay for property taken under the right of eminent domain.

The purpose of the *grand jury* is to limit the power of the federal government to prosecute citizens. A grand jury is a group of citizens selected to hear evidence of criminal activity and to determine if the person charged with the crime should be held for trial. They do not determine the guilt or innocence of the accused, the function of the trial or petit jury, but decide whether or not the evidence against him is strong enough to present to the petit jury. This portion of the 5th Amendment has not been made applicable to the states through the 14th Amendment and so many states do not have grand juries. In those that do not, the office of the district attorney issues the charges, called indictments. There has been discussion to the effect that grand juries are no longer useful and merely prolong the legal process, since the district attorney presents the evidence against defendants to them and the grand jury simply "rubber stamps" his decisions. However, unless the Constitution is amended to eliminate them, all felony indictments in the federal courts will still be issued by grand juries. Where states do use grand juries, however, selection of members of the grand jury must be on a racially non-discriminatory basis.[1]

The right to a grand jury indictment or a trial in the regular courts does not apply to servicemen on active duty. If a serviceman transgresses a military law, he is *court-martialed*.

The Supreme Court held in the case of *O'Callahan v. Parker*[2] that a serviceman may not be court-martialed for a crime committeed off his base in the United States against a civilian. The Court held that in case of such an offense, he may be tried *only* by the regular civilian courts as if he were an ordinary civilian and he may not be court-martialed either instead of or in addition to the civilian trial. Court-martial for a non-service-connected offense instead of a civilian trial by jury was held to violate the serviceman's rights under numerous provisions of the Bill of Rights as well as under general principles of due process of law.

Example

Peter Private, on active duty at a base in New York, murders Victoria Victim in her apartment in New York City. Peter may only be tried by the ordinary New York criminal courts and the Army may not court-martial him at all.

Crimes committed on military bases, even if non-military offenses, are tried by court-martial and not in ordinary criminal court.[3]

Example

Peter Private murders another soldier who has been dating Peter's girl friend. The crime occurs in the barracks where they both live. Peter is court-martialed.

The service of which a man is a member court-martials him and although he is guaranteed a fair hearing and protection of his constitutional rights, he is not guaranteed a jury trial.

A civilian employee or a dependent on a base may not be court-martialed, since the military has no jurisdiction over them.[4] If the crime is committed on an American base either here or overseas, the employee or dependent is returned for trial in the ordinary federal courts. If the crime is committed in a foreign country and involves a civilian of the host country, the dependent or employee will be tried in the courts of the foreign country.

Examples

1   Joe Dokes, a Private in the Army, and his wife hold up the Post Exchange at his base near London. Since this is a purely military matter, Dokes would be court-martialed and his wife would be returned to this country to be tried in federal court.

2   Dokes and his wife hold up a store in downtown London. They would be tried by the British courts.

The *double jeopardy* clause in the Fifth Amendment prevents either state or federal authorities from bringing the same person to trial more than once for the same offense after he has been acquitted by a jury. It is designed to prevent unfair harassment of a person by repeated attempts to convict him of a crime of which he has already been found not guilty.

Example

Nathan Nasty is tried for murdering his wife. The jury renders a verdict of not guilty. Once the verdict is given, Nasty may write a book about how he did it and no further legal proceedings may be taken against him.

If a defendant is convicted, appeals his conviction and the appellate court finds a legal error and orders a new trial, the defendant may not plead double jeopardy.[5] In this case, he is the one who initiated the appeal.

If the defendant has been convicted of a lesser charge at his first trial, however, he may only be tried for that crime at his second. For example, if someone is charged with murder and convicted of manslaughter, appeals that conviction and is awarded a new trial, he may only be charged with manslaughter at the second trial.[6]

If the accused is convicted the second time as well, it is not unconstitutional for the sentence to be longer than that handed down at the first trial. However, in that situation, the judge must give specific reasons for the sentence in order to avoid the appearance of retaliation against a defendant who was exercising his or her legal rights.[7] A single trial on two counts charging different crimes arising out of the same events which results in a finding of guilty on both is grounds for the judge giving two consecutive, not concurrent, sentences. This does not violate the defendant's right against double jeopardy.[8]

If the members of the jury cannot reach a verdict and the judge declares a mistrial, the defendant's rights against double jeopardy are not violated if he is tried again.[9] If, however, the judge dismisses the charges because of defects in the prosecution's case, the defendant may not be tried again.[10]

Example

A man was charged with grand larceny by false pretenses. A jury was empaneled and sworn, but before the case began, the man's lawyer pointed out that the date of the charge was incorrect. The trial judge ordered the charges dropped. The State later attempted to try the man again for the same event. The Supreme Court held that his rights against double jeopardy were violated.[11]

One act may constitute violations of both state and federal law. If so, the courts have held that two sovereign powers are involved and that each level of government may try the defendant and no double jeopardy has occurred.[12]

Example

John Criminal robs a bank. This is a crime under both state and federal law. He is tried in state court. Regardless of the outcome of that trial, he may also be tried in federal court. He has not been tried in the same court twice.

Double jeopardy also does not prohibit trials in two states if one event involved both of them.[13]

Example

A woman is kidnapped at gunpoint from the parking lot of a shopping center in State A. Eighteen hours later, her body is found in a ditch in State B, thirty miles from the shopping center. Medical evidence establishes that she was killed where she was found. State A arrests a suspect and he is tried and convicted of kidnapping. State B may try him for murder and his right against double jeopardy has not been violated.

A city, county, or municipal court is not, however, considered to be separate from a state court. Thus a person may not be tried twice in two different courts if both are instrumentalities of the same government.[14]

Examples

1 A seventeen-year-old was tried in Juvenile Court for armed robbery. He was found guilty and the judge concluded that he should be sentenced as an adult. He was, therefore, retried in adult court and again convicted. The Supreme Court held that his second trial violated the double jeopardy clause since he had been found guilty in his Juvenile Court trial.[15]

2 A member of the Navajo tribe was convicted in a tribal court and served his punishment. He was then tried for the same offense in federal court. The Supreme Court said that the second trial was not double jeopardy because the two were different jurisdictions.[16]

One act may also consitute more than one crime under state law or under federal law.[17] Two prosecutions in the same court for different offenses do not constitute double jeopardy.

Examples

1 Sale of two bags of cocaine to two buyers who enter the seller's premises together is considered to be two separate offenses and the seller may be tried twice.[18]

2 If more than one person is murdered in a shooting spree, separate trials for each murder do not constitute double jeopardy.[19]

3 An automobile driven by an adolescent struck and killed two small children. The teenager was cited at the scene for "failing to reduce speed to avoid an accident." A month later, he pleaded guilty and paid a $15.00 fine. The state then attempted to try him for manslaughter. The Supreme Court held that such a trial would not violate his right against double jeopardy if the state's case did not include elements of the offense to which he had already pleaded guilty.[20]

Where, however, the evidence to be presented at the trial of the second offense is the same used in the first, the second trial violates the defendant's rights.

Examples

1 A defendant was charged with committing a murder in the course of a robbery. He was tried for both murder and robbery and acquitted. He was brought to a second trial for robbery alone. The Supreme Court held that his right against double jeopardy had been violated.[21]

2 A man was charged with robbing a number of people who were playing poker. He was tried for robbing one and was acquitted. His defense was that he was not present when the robbery occurred. He may not be tried later for robbing a second poker player.[22]

3 A person was arrested for mailing a bomb that killed two people. He was tried for one murder and acquitted. His defense was that he had not mailed the bomb. He cannot thereafter be tried for the murder of the other person.[23]

4 A man stole a car. Nine days later he was arrested and charged with "joy-riding" on the day of his arrest. He was convicted. The state later tried to bring him to trial for car theft. The second prosecution was held to violate his rights against double jeopardy because the theft and the joy-riding were parts of the same offense for which he had already been tried.[24]

5 A driver was convicted of drunk driving after an accident in which someone had died. The defendant appealed his conviction. While the appeal was pending, he was indicted for manslaughter because of the death. This was held to be a violation of his rights of due process of law as well as of double jeopardy.[25]

By 1969, when the Supreme Court considered the issue, only five states' constitutions did not prohibit double jeopardy, but the Court held that as to those five, this guarantee was applicable through the due process clause of the 14th Amendment. Thus the same right acknowledged in the federal courts would be applied to criminal trials in all the states.[26]

The philosophy behind the clause of the 5th Amendment that prohibits compulsory *self-incrimination* is that the state and federal government must establish guilt of criminal acts by independent evidence, since no one should be required to testify against himself.[27] This right is designed to protect against the force of the courts themselves. This right is an absolute one and may not be abridged for any reason. Again we see the principle that in our legal system, the end does not justify the means. The operative word, however, is "compulsory." If a witness makes voluntary disclosures instead of claiming the right to remain silent, the government has not compelled him to incriminate himself.

Example

A professional gambler was indicted for conspiracy to "fix" an event. He objected to the prosecution's introduction into evidence of his income tax returns that listed his occupation as "professional gambler." The Supreme Court held that this disclosure was not compelled and could, therefore, be used in evidence.[28]

If a person is involved in any sort of investigation by law enforcement officials, he has the right to invoke this privilege. He must, however, claim that he would be incriminated by answering questions—that what he said would link him to a criminal act.[29]

Refusal to answer cannot be based on a statement that it would be embarrassing or that it would ruin one's reputation. Also, the only person one may refuse to incriminate is one's self.[30]

The privilege against self-incrimination applies only to compelled oral or written *testimony*. It does not apply, for example, to statements made to an informant in the same jail cell, as long as the cellmate just listens to what the accused says and does not question him.[31] It does not apply to statements volunteered to a policeman prior to an arrest.[32] For example, if a person walks up to a policeman on the street, tells him that God has told him to confess and that he would like the policeman to know that he murdered someone and buried the body under a tree, if the body is found under the tree and the person is tried, the statement may be admitted in evidence. In one case, for example, a man had been arrested for murder. He had refused to make a statement. A policeman remarked to a fellow officer in front of the man that he wanted to find the victim's body so that her family could give her a Christian burial. At that, the suspect told the policeman where the body was. The Supreme Court held that since the body would inevitably have been discovered anyway, evidence that the suspect knew where it was could be admitted.[33]

The privilege does not apply to books or records, whether they are in the hands of the person being investigated[34] or his or her accountant.[35] The privilege protects us from coerced testimony, not from volunteered testimony and not from coercion to produce existing evidence.[36]

Evidence obtained by forcible stomach pumping, blood tests, or physical examinations may violate the Fourth Amendment provisions restricting searches and seizures, but they do not constitute Fifth Amendment self-incrimination.[37] For that reason, if a person who has been arrested for driving under the influence of alcohol refuses to take a blood alcohol test, submission of that refusal into evidence at his trial is permitted and does not violate his right against self-incrimination.[38]

Rights under the Fifth Amendment begin when a person is questioned.[39] No influence may be used to induce admission of criminal behavior or commission of a crime. The person may not be frightened or threatened or promised a lighter sentence if he confesses. He must be advised by the police that he has a right to remain silent and that if he wishes to make a statement, it will be used in evidence at his trial.

A suspect must be advised that he has the right to confer with an attorney and that if he wishes to do so, he has the right to appointed counsel if he cannot afford one.[40] If he says that he would like to speak to a lawyer, questioning must stop and if it does not, any subsequent statements are inadmissible in evidence.[41] If a suspect remains silent, however, failure to tell him that his lawyer is trying to contact him does not violate this right.[42]

If a confession is completely voluntary, it may be used in evidence at trial, but if it has been coerced, not only may the confession not be used, but any information the police received by coercing a prisoner is also inadmissible.[43]

Examples

1   Joe is held in jail for three days and beaten by the police. They are trying to get him to admit involvement in a robbery. Joe finally tells them that he did it and the loot is buried under his back steps. Since the police would not have found the loot except by the use of unconstitutional activities, neither the confession nor the goods may be used in evidence at Joe's trial.

2   A man is accused of using a sawed-off shotgun to rob a cab driver. The accused is advised of his rights at least three times and asks to speak to his lawyer. While he is riding in the police car to the jail, one officer mentions to another officer that he certainly hopes the shotgun turns up soon—a child might find it and kill himself. The accused interrupts the conversation and tells them where the gun is. The gun is admissible in evidence at his trial, because the statement was voluntary.[44]

3   Statements made by a taxpayer in his own house at an interview with Internal Revenue agents were admissible in later tax fraud proceedings although his rights had not been explained to him. He was not in custody at the time.[45]

If a defendant does not make a statement or elects not to testify in his own behalf at his trial, a prosecutor may not comment on his refusals. Since one has the constitutional right to remain silent, adverse comment upon its exercise would make it worthless.[46] Where a suspect is questioned without being warned of his constitutional rights, however, those statements may be used on cross examination to attack the testimony he gives at his trial if he has voluntarily decided to testify. Even if the statements he made cannot constitutionally be used as a "confession" they may be used to demonstrate inconsistencies and conflicts between what he said at the police station and the testimony he has just given in open court.[47]

During an investigation, the prosecutor or a Congressional committee may grant the witness "immunity." This means that he will not be prosecuted for any criminal acts disclosed by answering questions. At this point, the self-incrimination privilege no longer applies and the witness must answer.[48]

If one person who has been accused of a crime is offered immunity in return for an agreement to testify against a co-defendant, failure to inform the jury of that fact violates the co-defendant's rights, since it affects the believability of the testimony given against him.[49]

Example

John Small and his partner were involved in a jewel robbery. The District Attorney suspects that the partner actually committed the theft and that Small knows where the jewels are. He may grant Small immunity. As long as the facts do not also constitute a federal crime, Small may no longer refuse to answer questions. At no time thereafter may the state take any action against him for his part in the robbery.

If the acts under investigation constitute a crime under both federal and state law, granting immunity only under one will not end the privilege.[50]

"Privilege," which is a matter of the rules of evidence, not of constitutional law, is the right of a person who occupies a confidential relationship to the accused to refuse to answer questions about him or his business. Normally, this right exists as to a defendant's physician, attorney, religious advisor and spouse. Usually, the only time any of those persons may be required to testify either to a prosecutor who wants a statement from them or to a grand jury or jury is where the defendant himself wishes to offer testimony by the privileged person. The Supreme Court has held in the case of *Branzburg v. Hayes*[51] that a newspaper reporter does not have either common law privilege or a right under the First Amendment guarantees of freedom of the press to refuse to answer grand jury questions about confidential news sources. He also may not refuse to disclose information from news stories that he did not publish. Even if the source of the news item was considered confidential information, the Supreme Court has held that he is obliged to reveal it if it is evidence of a criminal act. An accountant also has no privilege and must testify about a taxpayer's records he has prepared.[52]

The clause in the 5th Amendment pertaining to deprivation of life, liberty, or property without *due process of law* applies only to the federal government but there is a parallel clause requiring application of due process by the states in the 14th Amendment. Due process of law does not grant any specific rights such as the right to counsel. It means that the law must "play fair." It requires compliance not only with the outward forms of the law but with all that is meant by the ideas of liberty and justice for all.

There are two aspects of due process. Substantive due process means that laws which create rights, define crimes, or regulate behavior must be reasonable and not arbitrary. A law that makes some conduct illegal and provides for a fine or prison sentence for commission of some act must be restricting a truly anti-social act. The purpose of the law is, therefore, involved in determination of substantive due process.

Examples

1   A law which made it a crime to have red hair would be an unreasonably arbitrary law. Having red hair is not an antisocial act. This law would violate substantive due process.

2   Laws that provide penalties for murder are designed to prevent a genuinely anti-social act. Laws making murder a crime do not violate substantive due process.

Procedural due process, on the other hand, prescribes the method of enforcing or obtaining rights under the law. Procedural due process means that the process through which the law moves (the arrest, indictment, trial, verdict and sentence in a criminal case) must be fair.

Example

Using torture to extract a confession violates fundamental principles of fairness and justice and therefore violates the idea of procedural due process.

Due process, then, means that the law sets forth upon a course of action according to those rules and principles that have been established in our legal system for the protection of private rights.[53]

Our rights under due process are far more extensive than those we have with what we perceive to be relationships with "the legal system." Interactions with state institutions or private institutions receiving federal funds must also be governed by fairness. For example, a student in a state university medical school may not be dismissed for failing courses until there has been a suitable deliberative process within the school[54] and a severely retarded patient in a state institution has the due process right to adequate training to ensure his safety and freedom from restraint.[55]

In the context of civil litigation, due process also

encompasses a requirement of fundamental fairness. For example, the father of an illegitimate child who supports the child and has a "significant relationship" with him or her has the right to be heard when the child's mother's husband wishes to adopt the child.[56] In child-abuse cases, if the state wishes to terminate permanently the parents' rights to the children, the state must prove the charges by a fair preponderance of the evidence.[57] Anything less violates the parents' right to due process of law.

In criminal cases, in addition to the due process rights to which a defendant is entitled in the courtroom, after conviction and imprisonment, due process demands that he be treated fairly. For example, a prisoner has a right to a fair administrative hearing before he is punished for violation of prison regulations.[58]

In summary, requirements for substantive due process demand that the federal government (or states, under the 14th Amendment) or the institutions they support may not deprive any person (not just citizens) of life, liberty or property without good reason and in a fair manner. In our complex society, questions of governmental fairness are around us every day.

Examples

1   Does an elderly person who has lived in a nursing home for years and whose care is paid by the federal government have any right to complain if a social worker decides he should be moved to a different facility which is cheaper?[59]

2   Does a man who will die if he stops kidney dialysis, financed by the federal government, have any right to be heard about cut-backs in funding that will exclude him from coverage unless he can pay for it himself, where the nature of the disease means that he cannot work?

3   A widowed mother with two babies is entirely dependent on Aid to Families with Dependent Children. Does she have any rights not to give the name of a man with whom the welfare worker suspects she is having a relationship, since the man has no legal obligation whatever to support her children?

The last clause in the Fifth Amendment restricts the federal government's right of *eminent domain*, which is the power to acquire private property for public use, by requiring that the owner be paid the fair value of the property taken.[60] State governments also have the right of eminent domain, but the same restrictions apply. Cities and states may put restrictions on land use, such as enacting zoning laws which prohibit certain types of land use in residential areas without invoking the power of eminent domain.[61] Eminent domain only applies when the governmental agency seeks to remove ownership of the property to itself from private landowners or to transfer ownership for some public purpose.[62]

The property taken must be used in some manner that benefits the public and the owner must be paid its fair value. Determination of price is made in many ways, but it always requires some form of judicial process.

Sometimes, governmental use of its own property renders neighboring land owned by other unusable. In these situations, the government must pay the owner for the decline in property values.[63]

Example

Ann Sleepless bought her house thirty years ago. A year ago, the Air Force built a training base a block away. Jets land all day and all night, Ann can't sleep, her windows break, and plaster comes off the wall each time a landing plane flies over. If she is forced to sell her home and move elsewhere, the government must pay Ann for "taking" her home.

Amendment Six

In all criminal prosecutions, the accused shall enjoy the right to a speedy and public trial, by an impartial jury of the State and district wherein the crime shall have been committed, which district shall have been previously ascertained by law, and to be informed of the nature and cause of the accusation, to be confronted with the witnesses against him, to have compulsory process for obtaining Witnesses in his favor, and to have the Assistance of Counsel for his defence.

THIS AMENDMENT specifies procedural rights granted to persons charged with federal crimes, all of which have been made applicable through the 14th Amendment to state court proceedings.

The requirement of a *speedy trial* is designed to prevent indefinite imprisonment before trial. If not so restricted, the government could dispose of its critics by holding them in jail for years "awaiting trial" on ridiculous charges. This provision means only that the state or federal government may not purposefully and deliberately hold a person awaiting trial for an unnecessarily long time. In many areas the dockets of the criminal courts are very crowded and a defendant who is tried in his proper turn may not complain of denial of his right. The right is only abridged when the prosecuting authority deliberately delays a trial.[1]

Examples

1   Joe Blow, charged with a misdemeanor for which the maximum sentence is 10 days, is in jail awaiting trial. Since the courts are crowded, he waits 20 days for his trial. If he were tried in his proper turn, his right to a speedy trial was not abridged.

2   In the example given above, if men arrested two weeks after Blow were tried before him, his right to a speedy trial would have been abridged.

In the case of *Klopfer v. North Carolina*,[2] the Supreme Court held that the right to a speedy trial applied to state courts through the due process clause of the 14th Amendment. However, the Court reiterated its position that as long as a defendant was tried in his turn, mere delay in reaching trial due to an overcrowded court docket was not a violation of his constitutional rights.[3]

If a person is questioned about a crime but no further action is taken for several years, at which time the person is arrested, the right to a speedy trial is inapplicable. This right does not apply during a period in which a defendant is not under indictment or restraint.[4]

Example

A military physician was charged by the Army with the murder of his wife and two small daughters in their home on the base. After preliminary hearings, those charges were dismissed. Four years later, largely due to the efforts of his dead wife's parents, he was indicted for the murders by the ordinary civilian authorities. The jury convicted him and he appealed. The Supreme Court held that the four year delay was not a violation of his right to a speedy trial, because during that time he had no constraints on his freedom and no criminal charges were pending.[5]

Secret inquisitions by any branch of the government are repugnant to our judicial system. The right to a *public trial* assures that justice must be carried out under the eye of the citizens. The right to a public trial also includes the right of the press to attend pretrial hearings[6] and questioning of prospective jurors.[7] Although normally reporters and other spectators are allowed to observe all trials, many courts have refused to allow television or movie cameras in the courtrooms. This policy has been upheld by the Supreme Court on the grounds that a trial is not a sideshow and the equipment necessary for picture-taking can prove very distracting to those involved.[8] A defendant who wishes the court to be cleared of spectators may ask the judge to do so. In some cases, where a witness is obliged to testify to events which are very embarrassing and about which privacy should be assured, the judge may also clear the courtroom.[9] This is very often done when the prosecuting witness is called to testify in a case involving a sexual assault.

The verdict in all federal criminal trials must be rendered by a *jury* unless the defendant himself requests that he be tried by the judge alone. Juries in federal courts when they are conducting criminal trials are always composed of twelve people and most states require twelve-person juries in cases involving serious crimes. However certain traffic violations and other minor crimes are frequently tried in traffic courts by six man juries in many states and some state constitutions provide for less than twelve persons in all cases. The Supreme Court has held that in those states, having fewer than twelve persons on a jury does not violate the defendant's rights.[10] State laws in most states also require a unanimous verdict to convict a defendant, as is true of all federal juries. The Supreme Court has held that state statutes that allow jury verdicts of guilt by nine of twelve jurors are constitutional,[11] although a jury of less than six would deprive the defendant of a constitutional right.[12] The Court has also decided that lack of unanimous jury verdicts in those states that do not require them does not deprive defendants of due process of law or to trial by jury.[13] The Court did, however, draw the line at nonunanimous six-member juries and found them unconstitutional in trials for serious offenses.[14] Unanimous verdicts are still required, however, in all federal trials and in those states whose laws provide for them, and if the jury cannot agree, the judge usually orders a "mistrial" and the defendant may be tried again. The jury must be impartial, which eliminates those with any special knowledge of the case, any relationship to any of the parties involved or those with any special interests.

Example

John Smith is charged with the murder of Joe Jones. If Jones's widow were on the jury, Smith's right to an impartial jury would have been denied.

The 6th Amendment right to trial by jury in all criminal cases that would constitute jury matters in federal court is now applicable to all state trials, regardless of any state constitutional provision to the contrary, through this Amendment and the due process clause of the 14th Amendment.[15] The Supreme Court has held that a jury trial must be allowed in any case where there is a possibility of imprisonment for more than six months.[16] Except for some very minor misdemeanor charges, therefore, a state's failure to provide a defendant with the opportunity for trial by jury is considered to be a denial of due process of law and is therefore unconstitutional.

Example

Under the law of state X, drunk driving is a misdemeanor although the penalty could be a prison sentence for as long as ten years. The state constitution provides that there will be no jury trials for misdemeanors. Under federal law, any possibility of a ten year sentence would mean that a jury trial would be guaranteed. Henry Hiccough is arrested by state police and charged in state court with drunken driving. He is entitled to a trial by jury.

The Supreme Court has held that racial discrimination in the selection of jurors is unconstitutional.[17] A white male defendant, for example, has the right to indictment by a grand jury and trial by a jury from which blacks[18] and women[19] have not been systematically excluded.

One problem arising in jury trials is the question of prior knowledge by a prospective juror who has read about the case in the newspapers. There may be a distinct collision between 1st Amendment rights to freedom of the press and the defendant's right to a fair trial. If a newspaper has indulged in lurid reporting of a particularly revolting crime and keeps up sensational coverage day after day, it is quite likely that jurors who are called to hear the case may have arrived at firm opinions. Since only the evidence presented in court may be used as the basis of a verdict, this obviously affects the defendant's right to a fair trial. The solution of the collision of the rights seems to be self-restraint by journalists, most of whom have always been responsible reporters and citizens. In some cases where irresponsibility has prevailed, however, convictions have been reversed because of the prejudicial publicity.

The defendant is tried in the district where the crime is committed. Before the American Revolution, colonists charged with political crimes against the British authorities were taken to England for trial. This, of course, meant that the jurors were more sympathetic to the Crown, and was the basis for this provision of the Constitution. If local feeling in a sensational case is, however, running strongly against the defendant and he believes that he will be unfairly convicted, he may ask for a "change of venue," which is removal of the trial to another area. The right of change of venue belongs only to the defendant and may not be exercised by the government. A right to change of venue exists even in a misdemeanor case which is to be tried before a jury.[20]

One of the fundamental principles of criminal law is that the defendant must know why he is being tried or, as the Constitution terms it *"to be informed of the nature and cause of the accusation."* This prevents imprisonment for noncriminal acts such as criticism of government policy. In order to prepare his defense properly, a defendant is entitled to know exactly with what he is charged and the circumstances under which he is supposed to have done it.

In all criminal proceedings, the prosecution has the burden of proving criminal intent. A defendant never has to bear the burden of convincing a jury that he or she "didn't mean to."[21]

Example

John Smith is in jail for murder. The state must furnish him with the following information: (1) the crime with which he is charged—murder; (2) the name of the person killed; (3) when and where the murder occurred, and (4) by what means he is charged with committing it.

A prosecutor must also disclose to the defense prior to trial all material evidence favorable to the accused.[22]

The *right to confront and cross-examine* witnesses gives defendent the right to rebut their testimony. This right is guaranteed in all federal and state criminal trials[23] but is not guaranteed in legislative investigations.

While a defendant ordinarily has the right to be present in the courtroom throughout his trial and in most cases no proceedings can continue in his absence, if he is disruptive of the orderly processes of the court, he may be removed and the trial continued.[24]

"Compulsory process" is a subpoena to compel the attendance of the defendant's witnesses. If he had no way to force people to come to his defense unless they wished to do so, he might well be unable to produce an alibi or other defense at his trial. The prosecution has always had the power of subpoena. The defendant's right to compulsory process in order to obtain witnesses on his behalf is now applicable to state courts through the 14th Amendment. In the case of *Washington v. Texas*,[25] the Supreme Court held that a state statute that denied the defendant the right to subpoena a confederate in the alleged crime to testify on his behalf was unconstitutional for this reason.

Example

Bertie Bad and Attila Awful were arrested together, but tried separately, for the murder of Dora Dead. Bertie knows Attila did it by himself. It would be unconstitutional not to permit Bertie to subpoena Attila as a witness for the defense at Bertie's trial.

Since 1963 and the famous *Gideon*[26] decision, all persons charged with felonies are entitled to have a free, court-appointed *attorney,* if they cannot afford their own, in state as well as federal trials. Prior to that decision, a defendant in a state court was automatically granted counsel only in a capital case or if he were illiterate, very young or otherwise unusually unable to defend himself. In 1965 the Court handed down the *Escobedo*[27] decision which held that a person has the right to counsel at the time of his arrest if the charge is a serious one, in order to avail himself of legal advice on such subjects as his rights against self-incrimination and bail.

In *Argersinger v. Hamlin*[28] the Supreme Court held that no defendant could be sent to jail or a penitentiary at all unless he had been represented by counsel at his trial or had clearly understood what he was doing when he waived his right to be represented by a lawyer.

The right to counsel is also granted in some situations other than criminal trials. Persons who have been convicted of a crime and placed on parole or probation, for example, have the right to counsel at a hearing to revoke their parole.[29] Those persons charged with a crime who are committed to a mental hospital instead of being tried have the right to legal representation at the commitment hearing.[30] A person on public assistance whose welfare benefits are being terminated has the right to a hearing on the matter and to have counsel if desired, although the Supreme Court has not held that counsel must be provided for a welfare hearing.[31]

Counsel, moreover, must prepare and present an adequate defense. Inattentive or negligent representation of a client is not "effective assistance of counsel" and a defendant therefore is entitled to a new trial.[32] There are, however, limitations on what an attorney may do in representing a client. Firstly, an attorney is an officer of the court and secondly an advocate for her or his client. Therefore, no client, civil or criminal, may ever require unethical conduct from a lawyer even if it would result in a favorable verdict. For example, an attorney may not present testimony at a trial that he or she knows to be perjured.[33] Likewise, if a defendant is convicted and wishes to appeal, the attorney does not have a constitutional duty to present every issue on appeal that the client wants, if the attorney believes the claim to be frivolous or unsupported by the record.[34]

If a defendant wishes to represent herself, she may do so, but if she is being tried for a serious crime, most judges appoint a "stand-by counsel" in case the defendant needs help in compliance with courtroom protocol and procedures. As long as the stand-by counsel participates but does not interfere, the defendant's rights have not been violated.[35]

In addition to court-appointed counsel, if a defendant's sanity is an issue in the trial or if the prosecution introduces psychiatric evidence, the defendant is entitled to the services of a psychiatrist at public expense to assist in defense of the charges.[36]

In most civil litigation (i.e., suits brought by an individual) a party is not entitled to court-appointed counsel if he or she cannot afford to hire a lawyer. However, under the Civil Rights Attorneys Fee Act of 1976,[37] attorneys representing persons in Civil Rights actions are entitled to compensation from the federal government. This is true whether the attorney is in a fee-for-service private practice or works for a nonprofit organization such as Legal Aid.[38]

Basic rights of procedural due process also apply to children who have been brought before a juvenile court. The theory behind the juvenile court system is that a child should not be branded as a criminal or imprisoned and that he should be rehabilitated instead of punished. For this reason, a judgment of delinquency in a juvenile court has never been a "criminal conviction" and confining a child to a reform school is not a "sentence of imprisonment." Because the juvenile courts are not criminal courts, for many years they were not required to extend any specific constitutional rights to the children before them, although the child was entitled to a fair hearing. In the 1967 *Gault*[39] case, however, the Supreme Court decided that the right to counsel, the right to confront and cross-examine witnesses against him, the right to have notice of the charges against him and the privilege against self-incrimination must be accorded a child in a juvenile court. The Court based its decision on the theory that a child in reform school has been deprived of his liberty to the same extent as an adult in a penitentiary and that he should be no less protected by the Constitution.

A juvenile does not have the right to trial by jury, however.[40] His conviction must be by the same basis of "guilt beyond a reasonable doubt" that is required to convict an adult of a criminal offense.[41] Since children have a right not to be held in detention except for very serious offenses, the question of the right of a child to bail has never been decided by the Supreme Court although there are numerous state and lower federal court decisions allowing it. Generally speaking, courts will release children without requiring money bonds prior to a juvenile hearing unless the child is considered dangerous, and therefore the question is rarely presented squarely to a court. Most authorities, however, think that a child who is detained because his parents are too poor to provide bail would have an excellent case on denial of due process of law. Unless the child or the home situation to which he would return is dangerous, he should not be incarcerated prior to a determination of guilt.

The next constitutional issues that can be foreseen involving juvenile courts are the questions of whether a child can be convicted and sent to reform school for an act that is not a crime if committed by an adult. Such behavior as truancy, being unmanageable, use of vulgar language, "being idle" and "disorderly" or "smoking a cigarette in public" have been the basis for incarceration of innumerable children. Very few of these cases have been appealed, but eventually this issue will be determined by at least the states' supreme courts and eventually will probably be heard by the United States Supreme Court.

Amendment Seven

In Suits at common law, where the value in controversy shall exceed twenty dollars, the right of trial by jury shall be preserved, and no fact tried by a jury, shall be otherwise re-examined in any Court of the United States, than according to the rules of the common law.

THIS AMENDMENT gives a right to a jury trial in a suit for damages in some cases in federal court, but the Constitution nowhere requires juries in civil cases in state courts.

This right exists for cases originating in the common law. The common law, as opposed to statutory law (laws passed by a legislature) consists of decrees of the courts, some of which date back to the earliest days of English law, and legal customs, which go back to antiquity. The English common law that was in force at the time of the Revolution is still the basis of our law today except in cases where it has been altered by statutes or by decisions of the courts of this country. This amendment, therefore, involves cases based on previous decisions or custom and not on Congressional legislation. Many acts of Congress provide that disputes arising under them shall be tried by juries, but in the absence of such a requirement, one has no right to a jury in a statutory action.

Examples

1 A wreck case between citizens of different states is tried by a jury because it is a common law action and is not an action resulting from a statutory right.

2 A suit by a radio station against the Federal Communications Commission as a result of the revocation of its license is based on a statute—the Federal Communications Act. Unless the statute specifically provides for a jury trial, the station is not entitled to one. This Amendment in no way applies.

If the parties to any civil action consent, the case may be heard by a judge without a jury.

If rules in an individual district court provide for trial of civil cases by six member juries instead of the more usual twelve, the Supreme Court has held that the provisions of this Amendment have not been violated.[1]

Active duty military personnel have no right to sue the government for damages, whether for personal injuries[2] (such as medical malpractice in a service hospital) or violation of their constitutional rights.[3]

Amendment Eight

Excessive bail shall not be required, nor excessive fines imposed, nor cruel and unusual punishments inflicted.

THIS AMENDMENT, made applicable to the states through the 14th Amendment, permits a person to be free from detention between the time of his arrest and the time of trial, allowing him to prepare his defense more effectively than if he were in jail. Bail is an amount of money that the accused agrees to forfeit if he does not appear at the time specified by the court for the trial of his case. The only reason money is required is to insure the defendant's presence, and if it is set higher than an amount reasonably necessary for that purpose, it is "excessive." Bail is set by the judge, who considers such factors as the financial situation of the defendant, the gravity of the offense charged, character, and previous record. In cases where the death penalty may be imposed, bail may be denied, because no amount of money is sufficient to assure a person's presence at a trial in which he or she may be sentenced to death.[1]

Where a crime may be punished by a fine, an order of restitution to the victim, or by a prison sentence, it is cruel and unusual punishment to send an indigent to jail.[2] The Supreme Court has found that such an arrangement constitutes discrimination based on ability to pay. The court must allow him to pay in installments or make other arrangements to collect the money. Only those persons who can pay a fine and refuse to do so may be imprisoned in these cases.

Cruel and unusual punishments are those shocking to the conscience of the civilized world. They include inhumane, barbaric, or degrading acts.[3] A prisoner who is shot during a prison riot has not, for example, been subject to cruel and unusual punishment, but one who is shot for walking too slowly would be.[4] Punishment that is out of proportion to the severity of the crime is also considered cruel.

Examples

1 A sentence of 20 years for dropping a candy bar on the street would be cruel and unusual.

2 A sentence of 20 years for murder is neither cruel nor unusual.

3 A state statute provided for life sentences without possibility of parole for persons convicted of multiple felonies. A man was convicted of numerous charges of writing worthless checks, most if not all of which were for amounts under $100.00. He was sentenced under the statute. The Supreme Court held that "repeat offender" statutes that apply to nonviolent offenses are cruel and unusual punishment because they are disproportionate to the gravity of the offenses.[5]

4 In 1982, the Supreme Court held that a sentence of two consecutive 20 year prison terms and two fines of $10,000 each for possession of nine ounces of marihuana was not cruel and unusual punishment.[6]

Eighth Amendment rights are also violated by denying prisoners the necessities of life, including food, clothing, shelter, and medical care. Many cases have indicated that refusal to permit a sick or injured prisoner to have access to a physician is a violation of his rights.[7] In these cases, the prisoner may sue for monetary damages under the Civil Rights Act of 1871.[8] A prisoner who has been provided with negligent medical care in a federal prison has the right to bring a medical malpractice suit[9] but most states do not allow prisoners to sue.[10]

Imprisonment for the condition of being a narcotics addict is cruel and unusual punishment, since addiction is an illness, not a crime.[11] The same thing is true of imprisonment for being an alcoholic, but sentences for public, disruptive behavior caused by alcohol are not precluded. The disturbing behavior, not the condition, is being punished.[12] Most states' laws provide for the civil commitment to mental institutions, not criminal sentences to prisons, for persons with substance abuse problems.

Prisoners who are found so mentally ill that they cannot assist their counsel at trial and are therefore committed to mental hospitals are entitled to judicial hearings on the issue of their sanity. Although commitment is not a criminal process, the prisoner is entitled to counsel and, under the due process clause, a fair hearing. He may present evidence in his own behalf and to confront witnesses against him.[13] Persons who are committed to mental hospitals prior to a conviction of guilt may not be held indefinitely without some determination of the facts of the case.

Example

A defendant who was a deaf mute was charged with robbery. He could not communicate with his lawyer, so he could not assist in the preparation of his defense. The trial judge committed him to a mental hospital for an indefinite period. Since there was no cause to believe that he could ever improve, the Supreme Court held that his commitment violated his Eighth Amendment rights.[14]

When a person has been tried and found not guilty by reason of insanity, however, the period of involuntary confinement in a mental hospital may exceed the maximum sentence he could have received to the penitentiary.[15] His mental state must be reviewed on a periodic basis, but if he is still dangerous to himself or others or gravely mentally disabled, he may be kept in the hospital after a prison sentence would have expired. Persons charged or convicted of crimes and sent to mental hospitals have a constitutional right to medical and psychiatric treatment once they are there. Merely locking them away and "warehousing" them is a violation of their Eighth Amendment rights.[16]

In 1972, the Supreme Court held that the death penalty was unconstitutional in all cases in which it had been unfairly applied to defendants who were indigents or members of minority groups and was not used in cases where affluent or white defendants had been convicted of the same crimes. The circumstances of such discriminatory applications of the death penalty constituted cruel and unusual punishment.[17] Following these decisions, thirty-five states enacted new death penalty statutes and litigation about their constitutionality continued. Finally, in 1976, the Supreme Court, although not able to agree on a majority opinion, decided five cases which concluded that the death penalty might be constitutional in murder cases. A mandatory death sentence was, however, unconstitutional. To be acceptable, the sentencing procedure must provide consideration of the character and record of each individual defendant and his or her crime and the procedures must protect against arbitrary imposition of the death penalty.[18]

It is unconstitutional as a violation of the right against cruel and unusual punishment to execute a prisoner who becomes insane after he is sentenced to death.[19] Psychiatrists who work in prisons are, therefore, being asked to treat people so that when they are better, they may be killed. Many physicians in this situation have decided to refuse to see these patients, since they think such treatment violates their professional responsibilities as physicians.

It is also unconstitutional to sentence someone to death if he participated in a criminal act that led to a murder but was not actively involved in the act of killing. For example, if two men plan a robbery and one is in the car while the other goes into a store and shoots the owner while robbing the cash register, the man in the car cannot receive the death penalty for the owner's death.[20]

Although the defendant being tried in a death penalty case is entitled to a jury representing a philosophical cross section of the community, potential jurors who are morally opposed to death penalties in all cases and whose opinion would not be affected by the evidence they hear at the trial may be excluded from the jury panel.[21]

Executions must be "humane." A prisoner may not be tortured to death. Permissible means of putting a prisoner to death include electrocution, gas, firing squad, or lethal injection.[22]

Virtually no civilian crime that does not result in the death of the victim can now lead to a death penalty. For example, the death penalty clause of the federal kidnapping act was found unconstitutional.[23] Since the justification for the death penalty is theoretically retribution, it cannot be inflicted where no death occurred.

Amendment Nine

The enumeration in the Constitution, of certain rights, shall not be construed to deny or disparage others retained by the people.

THIS AMENDMENT reiterates the view of the nature of man and the government expressed in the Declaration of Independence and the Preamble to the Constitution. This philosophy is based on the idea that all human beings have certain rights with which they are "endowed by their Creator" and that they possess simply because they are human beings. Some of these rights, such as freedom of worship, are enumerated in the Constitution while others, such as "life, liberty and the pursuit of happiness" are not. This amendment is designed to protect all the basic human rights that are not specifically covered by another provision of the Constitution. Since it was difficult to determine what, if any rights, exist under natural law in addition to the ones guaranteed by other amendments, only recently has this amendment been frequently used as a basis for court decisions. In 1947, the Supreme Court held that a right to engage in political activity was protected by this amendment.[1]

The modern use of the Ninth Amendment as a protection of one of our basic freedoms, the right of personal, bodily privacy, began in 1965. In that year, the Supreme Court struck down as an unconstitutional violation of this Amendment and of the 4th and 5th Amendments as well, a Connecticut statute forbidding the dissemination of contraceptive devices or medications. The Court held that a married couple has a "right of privacy" that may not be transgressed by the government.[2] In 1972, the Court extended the right to access to contraception to unmarried adults, since it found that statutes restricting that right were in violation of both this Amendment and the equal protection clause of the 14th Amendment.[3] In 1977, the Supreme Court held that statutes making it a criminal offense to sell nonprescription contraceptives to minors were unconstitutional, since minors as well as adults had a right of privacy.[4] In 1978, Congress amended Title X of the Public Health Service Act of 1970[5] to provide that no federally-funded family planning clinic could deny access to contraceptives to adolescents and attempts[6] by the Reagan administration to require parental notification if a minor girl received contraceptives were declared unconstitutional.[7]

The Supreme Court has also used this Amendment to strike down state statutes restricting interracial marriage, holding that the right to marry is a "natural right."[8]

In beginning a series of cases that are without doubt the most controversial Supreme Court decisions in the latter part of the Twentieth Century, on January 22, 1973 the Court held that state laws restricting the right of a woman to have an abortion violated her right of privacy and the right of her physician to treat his or her patient as his or her best medical judgment indicated. In *Roe v. Wade*[9] and *Doe v. Bolton*[10] the Court found restrictions on a women's right to control her own body in this situation to be unconstitutional. The only valid restriction a state may place on abortions during the first trimester of pregnancy are that they must be performed by a licensed physician, just as is true of any other surgical procedure. During the second trimester, to protect the woman's health, a state may require that abortions be performed in clinics, as opposed to a home or other nonmedical setting,[11] but the state may not require that second trimester abortions be performed in a hospital.[12] During the third trimester, however, the state may restrict abortion except where the mother's life or health might be endangered by a continuation of the pregnancy.[13]

As soon as the Supreme Court's 1973 abortion decisions were handed down, many states enacted statutes requiring consent from a married woman's husband before she could obtain an abortion. These were struck down by the Court as interfering with the woman's right to make this decision.[14]

Other state statutes provided that an unmarried minor could not have an abortion unless her parents consented. The Supreme Court struck down the right of a parent to veto a girl's decision to have an abortion in several cases,[15] but has upheld statutes offering a minor girl the option of parental consent or a finding by a judge that she is mature enough to make this decision for herself.[16]

The Supreme Court also ruled, however, that if a state did not choose to pay for abortions under Medicaid, the federal program to provide medical care for the indigent, the federal constitutional rights to privacy of women who wished to have abortions but could not pay for them had not been violated.[17]

In 1986 the Supreme Court refused to extend privacy rights to homosexual relationships and held that there was no right to bodily privacy even if both parties were consenting adults and the acts were performed in private. Thus the Georgia statute making homosexual acts (and some heterosexual ones) a criminal offense was constitutional.[18] The Supreme Court has also held that there is no right of privacy in a prison cell.[19]

This Amendment was added because Alexander Hamilton believed the Bill of Rights to be dangerous. He took the position that listing certain rights throughout the other amendments and giving them specific protection would leave the government free to transgress any that had not been so enumerated.

Amendment Ten

The powers not delegated to the United States by the Constitution, nor prohibited by it to the States, are reserved to the States respectively, or to the people.

THIS AMENDMENT neither adds to nor subtracts from the powers of the federal government as described in the body of the Constitution and was merely designed to reduce fears that the new national government might someday seek to exceed its proper powers.[1]

As we have seen, the powers of the federal government are limited to those specifically enumerated in the Constitution or powers which may reasonably be implied from them. This amendment does not diminish the authority of the federal government to resort to appropriate action to carry out an otherwise constitutional power, regardless of the extent to which the use of that power might conflict with state power.[2] It merely reiterates the relationships already established between the states and the federal government. This amendment has been the cornerstone of states' rights thought, but it is clear that the words "to the people" mean, as the Preamble says "*We* the people", all the people of the United States.

Amendment Eleven

The Judicial power of the United States shall not be construed to extend to any suit in law or equity, commenced or prosecuted against one of the United States by Citizens of another State, or by Citizens or Subjects of any Foreign State.

THIS AMENDMENT was proposed by Congress to the state legislatures in 1794 and declared ratified by the President in 1798. It amends Section 2 of Article III, which provided that a state could be sued in federal court by one of its own citizens or a citizen of a different state, and was designed to protect the sovereignty of the state courts over state business.

A citizen of any state must sue a state government in the courts of that state, but he may appeal a decision from the state supreme court to the United States Supreme Court as outlined in Article III.[1]

Example

John Smith, a resident of Delaware, is a patient in a mental hospital in Florida. If he thinks that he is being illegally detained, he brings a petition for a writ of habeas corpus in a state court. If, however, his writ is denied and he appeals to the Supreme Court of Florida and his appeal is denied, he may then appeal to the United States Supreme Court as outlined in Article III.

This privilege of immunity from suit in federal court does not belong to political subdivisions of the state.[2] A city, county, school board or other municipal organization may be sued in federal court.

Example

Joe Doe, a resident of Virginia, is in New York City when he is involved in an accident with a *city* garbage truck. He may sue in federal court. If, however, it were a *state* police vehicle, he would be required to sue in state court.

Amendment Twelve

The Electors shall meet in their respective states and vote by ballot for President and Vice-President, one of whom, at least, shall not be an inhabitant of the same state with themselves; they shall name in their ballots the person voted for as President, and in distinct ballots the person voted for as Vice-President, and they shall make distinct lists of all persons voted for as President, and of all persons voted for as Vice-President, and of the number of votes for each, which lists they shall sign and certify, and transmit sealed to the seat of the government of the United States, directed to the president of the Senate;—The President of the Senate shall, in presence of the Senate and House of Representatives, open all the certificates and the votes shall then be counted;—The person having the greatest number of votes for President, shall be the President, if such number be a majority of the whole number of Electors appointed; and if no person have such majority, then from the persons having the highest numbers not exceeding three on the list of those voted for as President, the House of Representatives shall choose immediately, by ballot, the President. But in choosing the President, the votes shall be taken by states, the representation from each state having one vote; a quorum for this purpose shall consist of a member or members from two-thirds of the states, and a majority of all the states shall be necessary to a choice. [And if the House of Representatives shall not choose a President whenever the right of choice shall devolve upon them, before the fourth day of March next following, then the Vice-President shall act as President, as in the case of the death or other constitutional disability of the President.] The person having the greatest number of votes as Vice-President, shall be the Vice-President, if such number be a majority of the whole number of Electors appointed, and if no person have a majority, then from the two highest numbers on the list, the Senate shall choose the Vice-President; a quorum for the purpose shall consist of two-thirds of the whole number of Senators, and a majority of the whole number shall be necessary to a choice. But no person constitutionally ineligible to the office of President shall be eligible to that of Vice-President of the United States.

THIS AMENDMENT was proposed in 1803 and declared by the Secretary of State to be ratified in 1804. It supersedes Article II, Section 1, Clause 3. The bracketed portions have been superseded by Section 3 of Amendment 20.

In a Presidential election, a voter casts his ballot not for candidates for President and Vice-President but for a slate of presidential electors selected by the various parties in his state. Each state has the same number of electors as the total number of its senators and representatives.

Once the election returns have been counted, the electors with the majority of the state's popular vote are entitled to cast *all* of the state's electoral vote.

If a candidate received two votes less than his opponent, he would not receive any electoral votes, since "the winner takes all." For this reason it is possible for a President to be elected by a minority of the popular vote and a majority of the electoral vote.

Example

Mr. Smith and Mr. Jones are the Republican and Democratic Presidential candidates.

	SMITH (R)	JONES (D)
South Carolina 8 Electoral Votes	170,000	150,000
North Carolina 13 Electoral Votes	243,000	245,000
	413,000	395,000

Mr. Jones receives 13 electoral votes and Mr. Smith receives 8.

The electors meet in each state at a time specified by Congress—the first Monday after the second Wednesday in December—and cast their ballots. Their sealed votes are then sent to the Vice-President, in his capacity as President of the Senate. He assembles the House and Senate on January 6 and in their presence opens and counts the electoral votes and then declares the new President officially elected.

If there are more than two major candidates for either the Presidency or Vice-Presidency, it is possible that none will receive a clear majority of the electoral vote. In this situation, the House of Representatives elects the President from the top three candidates. Two-thirds of the members constitute a quorum for this purpose and each state has one vote. A simple majority vote in the House is required for election. If the same situation occurs in the Vice-Presidential election, the Senate elects him from the top two vote-getters, again by majority vote with one vote for each Senator, with a quorum being two-thirds of the Senate.

As a result of this method, it is quite possible that the House would not be able to break a deadlock. It is assumed in such a case that the Vice-President would serve as President until the House could decide. This assumption was made explicit in Amendment Twenty.

If the President should die or become disabled between the time of the popular election and determination of the electoral vote, the Vice-President would become President, just as he would if the President died during his term of office.

Twice in our history a President has been elected with a minority of the popular vote. The first time, in 1876, Hayes won over Tildon with a minority vote. In 1888 Cleveland, with a majority, lost the presidency to Harrison. There has been, from time to time, discussion about amendment of the 12th Amendment to insure that this cannot happen again. The usual proposal is that the electoral vote be counted in proportion to the popular vote instead of the current practice. In that case, in a state with 10 electoral votes, if Mr. X received 60% of the popular vote, he would receive 6 electoral votes and his opponent 4.

Amendment Thirteen

SECTION 1

Neither slavery nor involuntary servitude, except as a punishment for crime whereof the party shall have been duly convicted, shall exist within the United States, or any place subject to their jurisdiction.

THIS AMENDMENT was proposed and ratified in 1865. The first section of this amendment outlaws slavery, the ownership of one person by another, peonage, in which a debtor is held by his creditor to work out the debt, and involuntary servitude, in which one is compelled by force to work for another against his will, whether he is paid or not.

The courts have held that being ordered by a court to pay alimony,[1] being drafted into the service,[2] requiring a conscientious objector to work in a non-combat job,[3] or requiring welfare recipients to work on city jobs[4] are not involuntary servitude. In recent years, the courts have held that requiring a restaurant owner to serve all races, as provided by the Civil Rights Act of 1964, does not place him in involuntary servitude.[5]

SECTION 2

Congress shall have power to enforce this article by appropriate legislation.

The Congress in 1867[6] and 1909[7] passed laws implementing the provisions of this amendment. These laws specifically abolished peonage and made violation of the statute against it a crime.

Under the authority conferred by this Amendment, Congress passed the Civil Rights Act of 1886[8] that prohibited discrimination in the sale of real or personal property. This act remained virtually unnoticed until 1968 and the decision of *Jones v. Alfred H. Mayer Co.*[9] The black plaintiff was refused the right to buy a home in an all-white neighborhood and sued under the act. The court upheld his claim under the act and said that such a law was within the constitutional authority of Congress, derived from this Amendment. The following year in *Sullivan v. Little Hunting Park, Inc.*[10] the court considered a situation in which a black family, which had bought a house in a subdivision, was denied membership in a swim club composed of other residents of the neighborhood, although the former owner's shares in the club had been transferred with the house. The court upheld the family's right to membership and held that the swim club was not a private club. Thus the club was required to comply both with the 1866 Act and with the 1964 Civil Rights Act.[11] In 1973, the Court decided in *Tillman v. Wheaton Haven Recreation Club*[12] that a club similar except that shares were not transferred with home ownerships, was also covered by the 1964 Civil Rights Act. However, a "genuinely private" club may, if it wishes, have rules forbidding white members to bring black guests.[13]

In 1968, Congress enacted the Open Housing Act[14] under the authority of this amendment and of the interstate commerce clause. This act forbids discrimination in the sale or rental of housing unless a one-family home is sold by the owner. The court has held that the right to sue under the act is granted not only to a minority person who has been denied access to housing but current tenants who become aware of discriminatory practices toward others may bring an action because the tenants' rights of association also are being violated.[15]

Amendment Fourteen

SECTION 1

1 All persons born or naturalized in the United States, and subject to the jurisdiction thereof, are citizens of the United States and of the State wherein they reside.

2 No State shall make or enforce any law which shall abridge the privileges or immunities of citizens of the United States;

3 nor shall any State deprive any person of life, liberty, or property, without due process of law;

4 nor deny to any person within its jurisdiction the equal protection of the laws.

THIS AMENDMENT was proposed in 1866 and ratified in 1868.

CLAUSE 1   In 1857 the Supreme Court held in the Dred Scott[1] decision that if Negroes were not citizens of the states in which they live, neither were they citizens of the United States, since one must be a citizen of a state to possess national citizenship. This amendment was passed as a result of that decision. It creates a national citizenship independent of state citizenship and confers all rights arising from it on all people born or naturalized in this country and on all those subject to the laws of the United States.

Except for children born here to enemy aliens in wartime and children of foreign diplomats, all babies born in the United States have American citizenship. Children who are born to foreign nationals in this country usually have dual citizenship.

Children born to American citizens abroad are also American citizens by birth and may usually claim dual citizenship. A child who is born abroad of an American citizen and an alien is considered a natural born citizen. However, the section of the Immigration and Nationality Act of 1952[2] which provided that his citizenship might be lost unless he lives in the United States for a continuous five year period between the ages of fourteen and twenty-eight was upheld as constitutional by the Supreme Court in *Rogers v. Bellei*.[3] Children born outside this country to American diplomats, however, are solely United States citizens.

Examples

1 Baby Doe, born to an illegal immigrant, is born in New York. He is an American citizen.

2 Baby Doe, born in this country to an ambassador from another country, is not an American citizen.

3 Baby Doe, whose father is a member of the United States Air Force, is born in Paris. He has dual French and American citizenship.

A child born to aliens on a foreign ship in American waters is not an American citizen, but Congress has defined the United States to include Guam, Puerto Rico, the Virgin Islands, and the Northern Marianas.

CLAUSE 2   The "privileges and immunities" clause of this amendment means that rights which owe their existence to United States citizenship—that is those which are entirely derived from this Constitution or federal laws—may not be abridged by the states in any way. These rights, which are few in number, have been held by the Supreme Court to include the right to travel between states,[4] the right to vote in national elections[5] and the right to engage in interstate commerce.[6] Most of our rights consist of those which we hold as citizens of the states in which we live—the right to trial by jury, for example. This clause merely protects some of the basic rights which are more particularly described by another portion of the Constitution.

For example, the Supreme Court held that a state statute requiring lawyers who wished to practice within New Hampshire to be residents of the state was an unconstitutional violation of their rights under the privileges and immunities clause. The woman who sought to be admitted to practice lived immediately across the state line in Vermont. She was closer to the city in New Hampshire where she wished to practice than she was to a city in Vermont.[7]

This section forbids transgression of these rights by an action of the state, but is not involved in a transgression of the Constitution or federal law by a private individual.[8]

Examples

1 A state legislature passes a law requiring all travelers to pay a tax before they may leave the state. This is a violation of this clause.

2 Ned Nut, a private individual, decides he will go to the bus station and prevent anyone from leaving until they pay him $1.00. This does not violate this clause.

CLAUSE 3 As we saw in Amendment 5, in regard to actions of the federal government, due process of law means that the law must not be arbitrary in its subject matter and that it must be conducted with fairness in its procedure. Criminal laws, in particular, must not be vague or indefinite. This clause of the 14th Amendment, known as the "due process" clause, requires state actions to meet these requirements. Due process at the state level exists when laws operate equally and fairly on all citizens.

This clause has been the subject of more Supreme Court cases than any other. The Supreme Court, during its recent history, has greatly expanded the meaning of this clause. Criticism of the Court in the past decade has arisen from its willingness to consider more and more abuses by the states not formerly considered violations of this amendment.

Example

Considerable displeasure with the Court's restrictions on the right of state or local police to question a suspect has been voiced by law enforcement officials. Prior to the decisions which have been rendered since 1964, all that had been forbidden was physical or psychological intimidation of a suspect.

Because the rights covered by this clause are basic and fundamental parts of the rights of man, they are protected by the federal Constitution against abuse or transgression by a state. The procedural rights protected by this clause include the right to a fair trial, the right to counsel,[9] the right to a public trial,[10] protection against unreasonable search and seizure,[11] the right of confrontation of witnesses,[12] and the right against self-incrimination.[13] Laws which violate the freedom of worship, speech, press and assembly violate the basic principles of substantive due process which must be guaranteed by the states.[14] A judge must be impartial in order not to violate a defendant's right to due process. For example, the practice in many small towns of having the mayor, whose primary job is to locate revenue for the community, also sit as traffic judge, where findings of guilt mean increased income for the city, was held to violate basic due process.[15] In short, the rights guaranteed by this Constitution under Amendments 1, 4, 5 (except for the grand jury provision), 6 and 8 are so basic that they are protected by this clause against state transgression.

Due process also applies to other forms of legal action that are not directly covered by the Bill of Rights. For example, the Supreme Court has held that due process required a fair hearing prior to revocation of parole.[16] A person who receives public welfare assistance is also entitled to a fair hearing before benefits can be terminated,[17] but when the loss of assistance is not life threatening, as with disability payments, the assistance may be terminated prior to a hearing as long as there is eventually a meaningful, fair review process.[18] In both cases, the person is entitled to notice of the hearing, the right to counsel, the right to confront and cross examine witnesses and to testify and present evidence on his own behalf.

Examples

1 A state law which abolished a church which was not engaging in dangerous practices would violate due process of law.

2 A law which made it a crime to wear cosmetics on the ground that they were immoral would be so arbitrary as to violate due process of law.

3 Holding Joe Schmoe in the city jail for three years without bringing him to trial, advising him

of the charges against him and denying him bail would violate due process.

As we saw in Amendment Five, due process questions are complex and defining it requires a balancing of the interests of the individual and the State.

As was true of the privileges and immunities clause, this clause only involves state action, not action of private individuals.

Examples

1   As we have seen, denial of the right to a speedy trial is a violation of due process by a state.

2   Frank's next-door neighbor Hector gets mad at him and locks him in his basement for three weeks. This amendment has not been violated.

CLAUSE 4   The matter of primary concern to the authors of this clause was the prevention of state discriminatory actions against any group. It was particularly designed to eliminate discrimination by race or color. It is designed to prevent any person or group of people from being singled out for hostile legislation or action by the state government and means that all persons in the same situation (school children, for example) must be dealt with alike by the state.

Probably the most important cases decided under this clause are the school segregation cases. *Brown v. Board of Education*[19] in 1954 overruled the Supreme Court's 1896 decision[20] that as long as segregated facilities were equal, black citizens were not denied constitutional rights. *Brown* and later decisions have held, in essence, that the segregation of children in public schools solely on the basis of race, even though the physical facilities and other tangible factors may be equal, deprives the children of a minority or special group of equal educational opportunities and therefore amounts to a deprivation of equal protection of the laws. School districts both North and South did very little, if anything, to implement the *Brown* decision and the effects of years of delay meant that the schools in many parts of the country are still trying to solve racial problems more than thirty years after the decision. In attempting to avoid prohibited segregation without actually creating integrated schools, many school districts in the 1960's undertook to create "freedom of choice" plans, relying on community pressure to keep most black children from choosing white schools. Those plans were speedily struck down by the Court in *Green v. New Kent County.*[21] "Grade-a-year" plans were held to discriminate against those children in grades higher than those integrated.[22] Rezoning

school attendance lines was not considered constitutional[23] and neither were several attempts to divide school districts into two, each of which would encompass almost all of the children of one race.[24] One county in Virginia simply closed its public schools. Private schools were opened for white children, there were none for blacks. The Supreme Court held that if Virginia operated any public schools at all, each county had to have them.[25] Finally, in 1969 the Supreme Court ruled that the time had come to end dual school systems forthwith.[26] Busing was the principle means used by school boards to solve the problem of how to integrate public schools when children came from neighborhoods that were almost always all-black or all-white. When walk-in schools reflect racially imbalanced housing patterns, the only means of integration was to cross neighborhood lines. The Supreme Court held this in 1971 to be an acceptable means of eliminating dual school systems.[27] Innumerable protests followed both in the courts and in the streets, but the Court refused to permit any further delays in equalizing educational opportunity.[28]

All public facilities operated on a segregated basis violate this clause. This means that public housing projects, municipal recreational facilities and public transportation must be operated on an integrated basis.

Facilities such as public swimming pools may, however, be closed if a city does not wish to operate them on a racially integrated basis. As long as all pools are closed, unconstitutional discrimination will not be held to exist.[29]

Racial discrimination in marriage laws has also been found unconstitutional. In *Loving v. Virginia,*[30] the Supreme Court found state laws prohibiting interracial marriages to be unconstitutional. The same conclusion was reached as to state laws that made interracial cohabitation a separate offense unrelated to laws on fornication or adultery that applied to all citizens.[31]

The Supreme Court has held that race is simply not a permissible basis on which people may be classified. Thus a private university with racially discriminatory policies may lose its tax-exempt status.[32] A court may not remove custody of a child from a perfectly proper mother whose second husband happens to be black and give the child to the biological father on grounds that the judge disapproves of interracial marriage.[33] An affirmative action plan that protected the jobs of minority teachers while white teachers with more seniority were laid off was also a violation of equal protection.[34]

Reasonable classification of citizens, however, does not violate the equal protection clause. Laws that fix minimum wages for women and children have been held to be reasonable restrictions.[35]

Lower federal court decisions[36] which found state statutes excluding women from jury service unconstitutional were not appealed to the Supreme Court. Women now sit on juries in all states. Some states, however, require women to volunteer for jury duty instead of being subject to mandatory call as are men. These statutes have been upheld by the Supreme Court.[37] Discrimination by race in selection of either grand juries or trial juries is unconstitutional regardless of the race of the person being tried.[38]

Within the past fifteen years, a number of the Supreme Court's equal protection decisions have focused on the issue of discrimination by sex. The early 1970's saw cases involving the unconstitutionality of a state statute that declared a preference for the father, not the mother, as the administrator of a deceased child's estate[39] and a 1971 decision that probably seems obvious to us now, but that received much media attention at the time, holding that a corporation could not adopt a policy of refusing to hire mothers of preschool children if it hired fathers of preschool children.[40] Such discrimination in hiring was also held to violate the equal employment section (Title VII) of the 1964 Civil Rights Act[41] that forbids employment discrimination on grounds of race, color, creed, or sex. In 1973 the Court held that a married woman in the Armed Forces may claim her husband as a dependent for purposes of military benefits on the same basis that a male member may claim his wife.[42] Another case upheld a comparable worth program for employees of the State of Washington and found that female prison guards in a women's prison must receive equal pay to men prison guards in a male prison, even though the jobs were not identical.[43]

Some of the cases involving equal protection questions of classification by sex have removed special advantages held by women. An Alabama statute that made husbands but not wives liable for alimony was declared unconstitutional.[44] A Missouri statute that gave widows greater benefits than widowers was also unconstitutional.[45]

Classification by sex is not, however, always violative of equal protection. Excluding females from draft registration, for example, was upheld as reasonable[46] and a California statute that made men but not women subject to arrest for statutory rape was also upheld as not violative of equal protection.[47]

Recent decisions have held that job discrimination[48] by sex or sexual harassment in the workplace[49] are clearly prohibited by Title VII. State statutes forbidding sex discrimination in membership in private but nonselective organizations such as the Jaycees are also constitutional and do not interfere with male members' rights of freedom of association.[50]

Example

A young woman with an excellent record in law school was hired as an associate in a large law firm. Several years later, she was told that she would not become a partner in the firm and was terminated. She sued and demonstrated that only a few of the partners were women and that she was denied a partnership on the basis of her sex, not her abilities. The Supreme Court held[51] that she had a right to bring an action against the firm under Title VII of the Civil Rights Act.[52]

Within the context of education, Title IX of the Civil Rights Act prohibits discrimination by sex in any educational program, public or private, receiving federal funds.[53] This protection applies to faculty as well as to students.[54] Title IX has meant that neither men nor women may be denied access to educational programs thought to be designed for one sex or the other. Athletic programs for female students, for example, must receive adequate funding, space, equipment, and faculty if male students' programs have them.

Example

A state university open only to women had a college level program in nursing leading to a B.S.N. degree. A male registered nurse who worked in a hospital in the city wished to enroll in the degree program and was denied admission, although he was permitted to audit courses. To obtain a B.S.N. from any other school, he would have had to resign his job and move away. The Supreme Court held that single-sex public education violated the man's rights under the equal protection clause.[55]

Illegitimate children were, in former years, discriminated against by various state laws prohibiting them from inheriting from the estates of their fathers, mothers, or both. In 1986, after a series of cases dating back many years, the Supreme Court finally held that any statutory scheme of disinheritance of illegitimate children violate their rights to equal protection of the laws.[56]

An illegitimate child has the same right to support by his father as if he were legitimate, since the contrary would deny him equal protection.[57] Under the laws of some states, if the mother of an illegitimate child died, his father was held to have no right to custody as would have been the case if the parents had been married. The Supreme Court held in *Stanley v. Illinois*[58] that such laws denied unmarried fathers equal protection of the laws since other parents could not be deprived of their children unless they were found to be "unfit" in a judicial hearing. Needy illegitimate children may also not be denied state welfare benefits given legitimate children.[59]

A state which denied the right of appeal to persons who had been convicted of crimes but who did not have enough money to pay for the appeal has been held to violate equal protection of basic rights to the poor.[60] Transcripts must also be provided for those indigent persons who wish to appeal convictions of misdemeanors. The Supreme Court held in *Mayer v. Chicago*[61] that an Illinois Supreme Court rule providing for free transcripts only in felony cases was unconstitutional. State poll taxes have been held to violate this clause.[62] State statutes requiring persons who wish to run for public office to pay large filing fees before their names could appear on the ballot denies equal protection of the laws to poor persons who are otherwise qualified political candidates.[63]

A tax exemption for churches and charitable organizations has been held valid although a taxpayer complained that he was denied equal protection.[64] A school regulation forbidding married high school students from taking part in extra-curricular activities was held by a state court to be a reasonable classification.[65]

In the case of *Shapiro v. Thompson*[66] the Supreme Court held that state laws which established a requirement of a period of residency before persons could be eligible to receive public assistance were unconstitutional. The Court found that these laws unfairly restricted the basic right of individuals to travel from state to state as they might wish and that the laws violated the "equal protection" clause of the 14th Amendment by creating unreasonable classifications (residents and non-residents) among poor people.

Example

Pauline Poor, living in Mississippi, with her two children, is sick and cannot work. Since her husband has recently died, she decides to go live with her mother in California. When she arrives there, she discovers that she and her children cannot receive public assistance until she has lived there for a year. Meanwhile, her children are hungry. However, her sister Paula, who is in identical difficulties, has always lived with her mother, so her children are eligible for assistance. The Court held that this denied equal protection of the laws to Pauline.

Denying welfare benefits to needy aliens on the grounds that they have not resided in a state for a specified period also violates the equal protection clause.[67] The Supreme Court held that aliens as well as citizens were included in equal protection guarantees.

Equal protection of the laws also prohibits a state from withholding money from school districts that allow children who are illegal aliens to enroll. Since education is a fundamental interest, the children must be allowed to receive it.[68] On the other hand, it is not a violation of a child's right to attend public school if he is living away from his family solely to attend school in a particular district and the district requires tuition payments.[69]

The Supreme Court has held, however, that where a state funds public education with both state supplements and district revenues, thus resulting in school districts with lower property valuations receiving less income, the equal protection clause has not been violated. As long as per-pupil expenditures are equal within each district, if one school district in a state spends twice as much per pupil as another, the child in the poorer district cannot complain that his right to an equal education has been denied.[70]

While state colleges and universities may constitutionally charge higher tuitions to out-of-state students than to students who are in-state residents, the criteria for determining what constitutes in-state residency may not be unreasonably restrictive.[71]

The rights of handicapped persons are also protected by federal legislation enacted under the authority of the equal protection clause. The Rehabilitation Act of 1973[72] was designed to allow handicapped persons access to federally-funded educational and employment programs. The Rehabilitation Act, however, did not give the federal government authority to intervene in treatment decisions about handicapped newborns[73] and did not preclude state cutbacks in funding for medical care for low-income handicapped persons.[74]

In 1975 Congress enacted the Education for All Handicapped Children Act.[75] It covers children from three to 21 and provides that no handicapped child may be excluded from public education because of disability and that every handicapped child is entitled to a free, appropriate education regardless of the nature or severity of his or her handicap. All supportive services required to allow the child to be at school are required.[76] If the school district cannot or will not provide an appropriate educational placement within the district for a handicapped student, his or her parent may place the student in an appropriate private school and the school district is responsible for the cost.[77]

Although the right to vote is the subject of Amendment 15, the question of the validity of literacy tests has been raised under this clause. It has been held that the requirement that a voter be able to read and write at an adequate level is reasonable for the state to make. Literacy tests which are *fairly* applied to all who wish to register are constitutional,[78] but literacy tests designed to limit the number of Negroes or any other special group allowed to register are in clear violation of this amendment.[79] Some members of Congress felt that use of literacy tests in a discriminatory manner had been so prevalent, however, that the Voting Rights Act abolished them in states with an abnormally low percentage of voters. The 1970 Amendment to the 1965 Voting Rights Act,[80] however, abolished all literacy tests of any sort in any state. This provision was upheld by the Supreme Court in *Oregon v. Mitchell.*[81]

The Supreme Court decided the Reapportionment cases, the first of which was *Baker v. Carr*, beginning in 1962, under this clause.[82] In states with a rapid growth in urban areas and in which apportionment of representatives on the state-wide and Congressional level had not been revised to keep pace with the growth, serious malapportionment occurred. It was possible for a county with a population of 1,000 to have the same number of votes in the state legislature as a county with a population of 100,000. This obviously meant that an urban vote was only one percent as effective as a rural vote. The Supreme Court held that unless all the voters have an equal voice in the election of those who make the laws, equal protection has been denied. The court therefore ordered reapportionment of legislatures and Congressional districts within a state in line with the "one man, one vote" rule. The Reapportionment decisions overruled many previous cases that had held that the apportionment and composition of state or congressional legislative districts was a political question and as such would not be decided by a court.[83] These concepts continue to be applied in numerous reapportionment cases with the proviso that no plan for reapportionment is constitutionally permissible if it dilutes minority voting strength against the provisions of the 1965 Voting Rights Act.[84] Unless a proposed redistricting plan violates the Constitution or the Voting Rights Act, however, a federal judge must defer to the state legislature on reapportionment.[85] State legislatures continue to be reapportioned.[86] Local government has been realigned[87] and Congressional districts have been readjusted.[88] School districts may no longer restrict the right to vote in school board elections to parents and property owners.[89] The Supreme Court held in two cases, however, that watershed district elections may properly be restricted to voters who are landowners.[90]

SECTION 2

Representatives shall be apportioned among the several States according to their respective numbers, counting the whole number of persons in each State, excluding Indians not taxed. But when the right to vote at any election for the choice of electors for President and Vice-President of the United States, Representatives in Congress, the Executive and Judicial officers of a State, or the members of the Legislature thereof, is denied to any of the male inhabitants of such State, being twenty-one years of age, and citizens of the United States, or in any way abridged, except for participation in rebellion, or other crime, the basis of representation therein shall be reduced in the proportion which the number of such male citizens shall bear to the whole number of male citizens twenty-one years of age in such State.

SECTION 3

No person shall be a Senator or Representative in Congress, or elector of President and Vice-President, or hold any office, civil or military, under the United States, or under any State, who, having previously taken an oath, as a member of Congress, or as an officer of the United States, or as a member of any State legislature, or as an executive or judicial officer of any State, to support the Constitution of the United States, shall have engaged in insurrection or rebellion against the same, or given aid or comfort to the enemies thereof. But Congress may by a vote of two-thirds of each House, remove such disability.

SECTION 4

The validity of the public debt of the United States, authorized by law, including debts incurred for payment of pensions and bounties for services in suppressing insurrection or rebellion, shall not be questioned. But neither the United States nor any State shall assume or pay any debt or obligation incurred in aid of insurrection or rebellion against the United States, or any claim for the loss or emancipation of any slave; but all such debts, obligations and claims shall be held illegal and void.

Sections 2, 3, and 4 of the 14th amendment are now obsolete.

SECTION 5

The Congress shall have power to enforce, by appropriate legislation, the provisions of this article.

Section 5 was the constitutional authority under which the major portion of the Civil Rights Act of 1964 was passed.[91] This act outlawed racial discrimination in employment, public schools, public facilities, and private facilities engaged in interstate commerce, and provided federal court remedies for those denied the rights guaranteed by the act. It also outlawed unreasonable discrimination by sex or religion in employment. Although state laws may forbid racial or sexual discrimination in nonselective private clubs, in the absence of such a law, a private club with a state liquor license that not only refuses to admit black members but that refuses to allow its white members to bring black guests to dinner is not sufficiently connected with "state action" to have violated federal discrimination laws as to the black guest.[92]

Amendment Fifteen

SECTION 1

The right of citizens of the United States to vote shall not be denied or abridged by the United States or by any State on account of race, color, or previous condition of servitude.

THIS AMENDMENT was proposed in 1869 and declared ratified by proclamation of the Secretary of State in 1870.

Because the right to vote insures a citizen that he has a voice in electing people who will insure his other rights, the right to vote is the most important right of all.[1] This amendment forbids discrimination against citizens by denial of their right to vote on account of their race or color. The 19th Amendment gives women the right to vote.

This right applies to state and local as well as federal elections.[2] It applies to party primaries where the primaries are conducted under the authority of state laws.[3]

Article I, Section 2, gives the states the right to fix voter qualifications. This power, however, must not be used to deny the right to vote in contravention of this amendment or the 14th Amendment protections of equal protection of the laws and due process of law.[4] Reasonable qualifications imposed by the state for registration such as age and length of residence within the state are perfectly proper, but the courts have held for 94 years, since this amendment was ratified, that disqualification on the ground of race is not a proper classification.

SECTION 2

The Congress shall have power to enforce this article by appropriate legislation.

This section was the authority for the enactment by Congress in 1965 of the Voting Rights Act.[5] It provided criminal penalties for any official of a state or city who refused to permit a qualified voter to vote, for anyone who has intimidated a person who has or is going to exercise his right to vote, and provided further criminal penalties for destroying ballots already cast.

The act grants jurisdiction to the federal courts over the election practices of any states that violate this amendment. Congress took the position that if less than half the adults of a state were registered to vote, there was a reasonable assumption that discrimination was being practiced in some manner. If literacy tests were being unfairly used, Congress prohibited their use at all. In states or counties where less than fifty percent of the people of voting age were registered by November 1964 or had voted in the Presidential election of that year, the federal courts are empowered to suspend literacy tests and require that prospective voters be registered without any determination at all of literacy. Under the Voting Rights Act as it has been amended and strengthened in 1975 and 1982, today no literacy tests at all may be given. The Act now covers the entire nation. In particular, in any area in which 10% of the population does not use English as its first language, all provisions of the Act now apply. Federal voting registrars may be sent by the federal courts to these states to register voters and supervise elections. The Supreme Court upheld the constitutionality of the original act in 1966 in a suit filed under the Court's original jurisdiction by the state of South Carolina.[6]

In the case of *Gaston County, North Carolina v. United States*,[7] the Supreme Court held that literacy tests are unconstitutional in states where a segregated school system had deprived blacks now of voting age of equal educational opportunity even if the test is not specifically designed to discriminate against prospective black voters. The court held that in those areas where segregated schools had meant inferior educational opportunities for blacks, even equal application of literacy tests would abridge their 15th Amendment guarantees because their inferior educations in turn denied them an equal chance to pass the tests. Thus, even impartial administration of literacy tests in those areas where black citizens had been systematically deprived of the educational opportunities granted to whites violates the "equal protection" clause of the 14th Amendment, the 15th Amendment and the Voting Rights Act of 1965.[8] The 1970 Amendment to the 1965 Voting Rights Act,[9] however, abolished all literacy tests of any sort in any state. This provision was upheld by the Supreme Court in *Oregon v. Mitchell*.[10] The Supreme Court held in 1973 that reapportionment of state legislatures and congressional districts must be done in such a way that the votes of blacks or other minority groups are not diluted by the process.[11]

Other irrelevant criteria for voter registration are also unconstitutional. For example, a state statute that prohibits persons convicted of misdemeanors—minor crimes, for which little or no jail sentence may be imposed—from voting was a violation of this Amendment and of the equal protection provision of the 14th Amendment.[12]

Amendment Sixteen

The Congress shall have power to lay and collect taxes on incomes, from whatever source derived, without apportionment among the several States, and without regard to any census or enumeration.

THIS AMENDMENT was proposed to the state legislatures in 1909 and proclaimed ratified in 1913.

The Supreme Court in the *Pollock*[1] case in 1895 declared income taxes unconstitutionally in conflict with the "direct tax" provisions of Article I, Section 2, Clause 3, and Article I, Section 9, Clause 4. The court held in that case that taxes on income must be apportioned among the states. This amendment, adopted to overcome that decision, permits the Congress to levy direct taxes on citizens' income from all sources.

Amendment Seventeen

The Senate of the United States shall be composed of two Senators from each State, elected by the people thereof, for six years; and each Senator shall have one vote. The electors in each State shall have the qualifications requisite for electors of the most numerous branch of the State legislatures.

When vacancies happen in the representation of any State in the Senate, the executive authority of such State shall issue writs of election to fill such vacancies: Provided, That the legislature of any State may empower the executive thereof to make temporary appointments until the people fill the vacancies by election as the legislature may direct.

This amendment shall not be so construed as to affect the election or term of any Senator chosen before it becomes valid as part of the Constitution.

THIS AMENDMENT was proposed by Congress to the state legislatures in 1912 and proclaimed ratified in 1913.

This amendment supersedes the portion of Article I, Section 3, which provided for the election of United States Senators by state legislatures. It establishes the direct election of Senators in the same manner as the election of Representatives. It also provides for an appointment until the next election of a Senator by the governor of a state in which a Senate vacancy has occurred.

Amendment Eighteen

[1 After one year from the ratification of this article the manufacture, sale, or transportation of intoxicating liquors within, the importation thereof into, or the exportation thereof from the United States and all territory subject to the jurisdiction thereof for beverage purposes is hereby prohibited.

[2 The Congress and the several States shall have concurrent power to enforce this article by appropriate legislation.

[3 This article shall be inoperative unless it shall have been ratified as an amendment to the Constitution by the legislatures of the several States, as provided in the Constitution, within seven years from the date of the submission hereof to the States by the Congress.]

> THIS AMENDMENT was proposed in 1917 and declared ratified in 1919. It was repealed by the 21st Amendment in 1933.

Amendment Nineteen

The right of citizens of the United States to vote shall not be denied or abridged by the United States or by any State on account of sex.

Congress shall have power to enforce this article by appropriate legislation.

THIS AMENDMENT was proposed in 1919 and declared ratified in 1920. It was rejected by the states of Alabama, Georgia, Louisiana, Maryland, Mississippi, South Carolina and Virginia.

This amendment gave women the right to vote subject to state voting requirements, which again could not transgress the 14th and 15th Amendments. A literacy test given to women but not to men was a violation of this amendment.[1] It did not give women the right to serve on juries,[2] and it also did not impose upon the states a requirement that women be eligible for public office.[3] All states, however, have now enacted their own legislation allowing women to serve on juries and, of course, to serve in public office.

The passage of the Nineteenth Amendment was the first major accomplishment of the women's movement. In recent years, the Equal Rights Amendment has been equally important to the present generation of men and women who are politically active about women's issues. The ERA was overwhelmingly passed by both Houses of Congress, but failed by three states to be ratified by three-fourths of the state legislatures. The issue is far from over, however, and plans to try again are still very much alive.

Amendment Twenty

SECTION 1

The terms of the President and Vice President shall end at noon on the 20th day of January, and the terms of Senators and Representatives at noon on the 3d day of January, of the years in which such terms would have ended if this article had not been ratified; and the terms of their successors shall then begin.

SECTION 2

The Congress shall assemble at least once in every year, and such meeting shall begin at noon on the 3d of January, unless they shall by law appoint a different day.

SECTION 3

If, at the time fixed for the beginning of the term of the President, the President elect shall have died, the Vice President elect shall become President. If a President shall not have been chosen before the time fixed for the beginning of his term, or if the President elect shall have failed to qualify, then the Vice President elect shall act as President until a President shall have qualified; and the Congress may by law provide for the case wherein neither a President elect nor a Vice President elect shall have qualified, declaring who shall then act as President, or the manner in which one who is to act shall be selected, and such person shall act accordingly until a President or Vice President shall have qualified.

SECTION 4

The Congress may by law provide for the case of the death of any of the persons from whom the House of Representatives may choose a President whenever the right of choice shall have devolved upon them, and for the case of the death of any of the persons from whom the Senate may choose a Vice President whenever the right of choice shall have devolved upon them.

SECTION 5

Sections 1 and 2 shall take effect on the 15th day of October following the ratification of this article.

SECTION 6

This article shall be inoperative unless it shall have been ratified as an amendment to the Constitution by the legislatures of three-fourths of the several States within seven years from the date of its submission.

THIS AMENDMENT was proposed in 1932 and declared ratified in 1933.

Until this amendment was ratified and superseded part of Article I, Section 4, a newly-elected President and Congress did not assume their offices until March after the elections in November. Since Congress convened in December, this left defeated officials to carry out the legislative and executive business of the government. This was known as a "lame duck" session.

When the date for the assembly of Congress was changed to January, it meant that the new Congressmen took their seats at once. Since the aboli-tion of the December term of Congress, the old session now adjourns before the elections in November and the new session begins in January.

Section 3 was made necessary by a problem caused by Amendment Twelve. Since the names of the three top vote-getters in a Presidential race were to be sent to the House in cases where no one was a majority winner in the Electoral College and each state was given only one vote, it was possible that none of the three could get a majority and a deadlock would occur. This Section makes clear that in that situation, the Vice-President would serve until the House could finally elect someone by a majority.

Amendment Twenty-One

SECTION 1

The eighteenth article of amendment to the Constitution of the United States is hereby repealed.

THIS AMENDMENT was proposed in 1933 and declared ratified the same year. It repealed the 18th Amendment and was rejected by South Carolina.

SECTION 2

The transportation or importation into any State, Territory, or possession of the United States for delivery or use therein of intoxicating liquors, in violation of the laws thereof, is hereby prohibited.

Section 2 of this Amendment gives the states full powers to enact their own laws regarding the sale of alcohol within their own boundaries. A state is constitutionally empowered to forbid any sale of alcohol if it wishes.[1]

For example, a California alcohol control board regulation forbidding "sexually explicit" live entertainment or films in places where liquor was sold was recently upheld even though the Supreme Court found that the forbidden activities did not necessarily meet the legal definition of obscenity. The court held that the state had the right to make this type of regulation under this Amendment, even if the activities ordinarily would be protected by the First Amendment.[2]

SECTION 3

This article shall be inoperative unless it shall have been ratified as an amendment to the Constitution by conventions in the several States, as provided in the Constitution, within seven years from the date of the submission hereof to the States by the Congress.

This is the only Amendment that has ever been ratified by conventions instead of by the state legislatures.

Amendment Twenty-Two

SECTION 1

No person shall be elected to the office of the President more than twice, and no person who has held the office of President, or acted as President, for more than two years of a term to which some other person was elected President shall be elected to the office of the President more than once. But this Article shall not apply to any person holding the office of President when this Article was proposed by the Congress, and shall not prevent any person who may be holding the office of President, or acting as President, during the term within which this Article becomes operative from holding the office of President or acting as President during the remainder of such term.

SECTION 2

This article shall be inoperative unless it shall have been ratified as an amendment to the Constitution by the legislatures of three-fourths of the several States within seven years from the date of its submission to the States by the Congress.

THIS AMENDMENT was proposed in 1947 and declared ratified in 1951.

This amendment prevents election of anyone to the Presidency for more than two terms. The only President who ever served more than two terms was Franklin D. Roosevelt, who died during his fourth term of office.

However, it is possible for a Vice President who succeeds to the Presidency as a result of the death of the President to serve as many as ten years, or two and one-half terms. If the Vice President succeeds to the Presidency for two years or less, he may then be elected for two terms.

Example

President Johnson served one year of President Kennedy's term. He was elected in 1964 and was eligible to run again in 1968. If he had chosen to run and had been re-elected, he would, at the expiration of his second term, have served a total of nine years.

Amendment Twenty-Three

SECTION 1

The District constituting the seat of Government of the United States shall appoint in such manner as the Congress may direct:

A number of electors of President and Vice President equal to the whole number of Senators and Representatives in Congress to which the District would be entitled if it were a State, but in no event more than the least populous State; they shall be in addition to those appointed by the States, but they shall be considered, for the purposes of the election of President and Vice President, to be electors appointed by a State; and they shall meet in the District and perform such duties as provided by the twelfth article of amendment.

SECTION 2

The Congress shall have power to enforce this article by appropriate legislation.

THIS AMENDMENT, which was proposed in 1960 and ratified in 1961, gives residents of the District of Columbia the right to vote for the President and Vice President. Congress has the power to establish voter requirements such as residency within the District, but these powers must be exercised in accordance with the various constitutional provisions protecting voting rights. The District has as many electoral votes as the state with the smallest population. Since all states have at least two Senators and one Representative, the District will always have at least three electoral votes.

Amendment Twenty-Four

SECTION 1

The right of citizens of the United States to vote in any primary or other election for President or Vice President, for electors for President or Vice President, or for Senator or Representative in Congress, shall not be denied or abridged by the United States or any State by reason of failure to pay any poll tax or other tax.

SECTION 2

The Congress shall have power to enforce this article by appropriate legislation.

THIS AMENDMENT was proposed in 1962 and ratified in 1964.

The purpose of the amendment was to prevent either the states or the federal government from impairing the right to vote in federal elections by requiring the payment of any tax.

Subsequent to the ratification of this amendment, although it did not affect poll tax requirements for state elections, the Supreme Court has declared *any* poll tax to be unconstitutional.[1] The Court held that the right to vote is so basic to our society that its exercise should never be made dependent on the payment of money. Such payments were held to violate the equal protection clause of the 14th Amendment.

Amendment Twenty-Five

SECTION 1

In case of the removal of the President from office or of his death or resignation, the Vice President shall become President.

SECTION 2

Whenever there is a vacancy in the office of the Vice President, the President shall nominate a Vice President who shall take office upon confirmation by a majority vote of both Houses of Congress.

SECTION 3

Whenever the President transmits to the President pro tempore of the Senate and the Speaker of the House of Representatives his written declaration that he is unable to discharge the powers and duties of his office, and until he transmits to them a written declaration to the contrary, such powers and duties shall be discharged by the Vice President as Acting President.

SECTION 4

Whenever the Vice President and a majority of either the principal officers of the executive departments or of such other body as Congress may by law provide, transmit to the President pro tempore of the Senate and the Speaker of the House of Representatives their written declaration that the President is unable to discharge the powers and duties of his office, the Vice President shall immediately assume the powers and duties of the office as Acting President.

Thereafter, when the President transmits to the President pro tempore of the Senate and the Speaker of the House of Representatives his written declaration that no inability exists, he shall resume the powers and duties of his office unless the Vice President and a majority of either the principal officers of the executive department or of such other body as Congress may by law provide, transmit within four days to the President pro tempore of the Senate and the Speaker of the House of Representatives their written declaration that the President is unable to discharge the powers and duties of his office. Thereupon Congress shall decide the issue, assembling within forty-eight hours for that purpose if not in session. If the Congress, within twenty-one days after receipt of the latter written declaration, or if Congress is not in session, within twenty-one days after Congress is required to assemble, determines by two-thirds vote of both Houses that the President is unable to discharge the powers and duties of his office, the Vice President shall continue to discharge the same as Acting President; otherwise, the President shall resume the powers and duties of his office.

THIS AMENDMENT was proposed to the states in 1965 and ratified in 1967.

This amendment provides that a President who considers himself for any reason unable to perform his duties may notify the Speaker of the House and the President pro tempore of the Senate of his disability. The Vice President would then become Acting President until the President notifies the same officials of his recovery.

If the President is unwilling or unable to make such a notification and the Vice President and the Cabinet believe that he is unable to carry out his duties, they may notify the same officials of the situation, and the Vice President again becomes Acting President. When the President informs the Speaker and the President pro tem that he has recovered, he resumes his duties unless the Vice President and a majority of the Cabinet still feel that he is too ill. In that case, they make a declaration to that effect to the Speaker and the President pro tem and within 48 hours the question is submitted to Congress. Within 21 days Congress must decide whether or not the President has recovered, and a vote that the President is still disabled must be carried by a two-thirds majority vote of both Houses. If the two-thirds vote fails, the President automatically resumes his duties.

This amendment will fill the gap in constitutional law that occurs whenever a President is ill, and provides for the situation in which the President might be severely disabled, mentally or otherwise, but would refuse to acknowledge his impairment.

This does not remove the office or title of President from the elected official. The Vice President serves as Acting President only while discharging the Presidential duties.

George Bush became the first "acting president" under this Amendment when these provisions were invoked for a few hours during President Reagan's 1985 cancer surgery.

Section 2 provides that if the office of the Vice-President is vacated, either by succession to the Presidency upon the death of the President or by the death or resignation of the Vice-President, the President may appoint a Vice-President whose nomination will be confirmed by a majority vote of both houses of Congress.

Amendment Twenty-Six

SECTION 1

The right of citizens of the United States, who are eighteen years of age or older, to vote shall not be denied or abridged by the United States or by any State on account of age.

SECTION 2

The Congress shall have power to enforce this article by appropriate legislation.

THE 1970 AMENDMENT to the Voting Rights Act of 1965[1] allowed eighteen year olds to vote in all elections. The Supreme Court, however, in *Oregon v. Mitchell*[2] declared that Congress was without authority to set the voting age in state or local elections by use of an ordinary statute. That section of the Act permitting eighteen-year-olds to vote in federal elections was, however, upheld. The result was that eighteen year olds were enfranchised in some elections but not in others.

This Amendment was introduced in Congress in January, 1971, almost immediately after the Supreme Court decision. It received approval of both House and Senate by March, 1971 and was ratified by the required number of states by the end of June, 1971. This Amendment was ratified in less time than any other in American history.

Eighteen year olds may now register and vote in any and all elections in this country.

Table of Cases and Statutes

★

66 *Palko v. Connecticut*, 302 U. S. 319 (1937).

67 *DeJonge v. Oregon*, 299 U. S. 353 (1937).

68 *Herndon v. Lowry*, 301 U. S. 242 (1937).

69 *Senn v. Tile Layers' Union*, 301 U. S. 468 (1937).

70 *Hague v. C.I.O.*, 307 U. S. 496 (1939).

71 *Cantwell v. Connecticut*, 310 U. S. 296 (1940).

72 *Thornhill v. Alabama*, 310 U. S. 88 (1940).

73 *Lovell v. Griffin*, 303 U. S. 444 (1938).

74 *West Virginia State Bd. of Education v. Barnette*, 319 U. S. 624 (1943).

75 *Bridges v. California*, 314 U. S. 252 (1941).

76 *U. S. v. Lovett*, 328 U. S. 303 (1946).

77 *Brown v. Board of Education*, 347 U. S. 483 (1954).

78 *Missouri ex rel. Gaines v. Canada*, 305 U. S. 337 (1938).

79 *Sweatt v. Painter*, 339 U. S. 629 (1950).

80 *McLaurin v. Oklahoma State Regents*, 339 U. S. 637 (1950).

81 *Smith v. Allwright*, 321 U. S. 649 (1944).

82 *Mitchell v. U. S.*, 313 U. S. 80 (1941).

83 *Henderson v. U. S.*, 339 U. S. 816 (1950).

84 *Shelley v. Kraemer*, 334 U. S. 1 (1948).

85 *U. S. v. Curtiss-Wright Export Corp.*, 299 U. S. 304 (1936).

86 *Yakus v. U. S.*, 321 U. S. 414 (1944).

87 *Korematsu v. U. S.*, 323 U. S. 214 (1944).

88 *Ex parte Quirin*, 317 U. S. 1 (1942).

89 *In re Yamashita*, 327 U. S. 1 (1946).

90 *Cramer v. U. S.*, 325 U. S. 1 (1945).

91 *Haupt v. U. S.*, 330 U. S. 631 (1947).

92 *Youngstown Sheet & Tube Co. v. Sawyer*, 343 U. S. 579 1952).

93 Smith Act, 18 U.S.C.A. § 2385.

94 *American Communications Ass'n v. Douds*, 339 U. S. 382 1950).

95 *Dennis v. U. S.*, 341 U. S. 494 (1951).

96 *Wieman v. Updegraff*, 344 U. S. 183 (1952).

97 *Terminiello v. Chicago*, 337 U. S. 1 (1949).

98 *Roth v. U. S.*, 354 U. S. 476 (1957).

99 *Burstyn v. Wilson*, 343 U. S. 195 (1952).

100 *Everson v. Board of Education*, 330 U. S. 1 (1947).

101 *McCollum v. Board of Education*, 333 U. S. 203 (1948).

Preamble

1 *McCulloch v. Maryland*, 4 Wheat. 316 (1819).

2 *Orleans Parish School Board v. Bush*, 188 F. Supp. 916 (1960), Affirmed 365 U. S. 569 (1961).

3 *Jacobson v. Massachusetts*, 197 U. S. 11 (1905).

Article One

1 *Youngstown Sheet & Tube Co. v. Sawyer*, 343 U.S. 579 (1952).

2 *Bowsher v. Synar*, 478 U.S.106 sct 3181, 92 L Ed 2d 583 (1986).

3 *Wiley v. Sinkler*, 179 U.S. 58 (1900).

4 *Commonwealth ex rel Dummit v. O'Connell*, 298 Ky 44 (1944).

5 *Powell v. McCormack*, 395 U.S. 486 (1969).

6 *Roudebush v. Hartke*, 405 U.S. 15 (1972).

7 *Shub v. Simpson*, 196 Md 177 (1950).

8 *Yellen v. U.S.*, 374 109 (1963).

9 *U.S. v. Grumman*, 227 F Supp 227 (DC DC 1964).

10 *U.S. v. Johnson*, 383 U.S. 169 (1966).

11 *U.S. v. Brewster*, 408 U.S. 501 (1972).

12 *Gravel v. U.S.*, 408 U.S. 606 (1972).

13 *Barsky v. U.S.*, 167 F 2d 241 (1948).

14 *Yellin v. U.S.*, 374 U.S. 109 (1963).

15 *Immigration and Naturalization Service v. Chada*, 462 U.S. 919, 1983.

16 *Rostker v. Goldberg*, 448 U.S. 1306, 1981.

17 *New York v. U.S.*, 326 U.S. 572 (1946).

18 *McCulloch v. Maryland*, 17 U.S. 316 (1819).

19 *First Agricultural National Bank v. State Tax Commission*, 392 U.S. 339 (1968).

20 *NLRB v. Carlisle Lumber Co.*, 94 F 2d 138 (1938).

21 *Pardin v. Terminal Ry. of Alabama*, 377 U.S. 184 (1964).

22 *Hillsborough County v. Automated Medical Laboratories, Inc.*, 471 U.S. 307 (1985).

23 *Hisao Murata v. Acheson*, 99 F Supp 591 (1951).

24 92 Stat 2549.

25 *Northern Pipeline Construction Co. v. Marathon Pipeline Co.*, 458 U.S. 457 (1982).

26 *Harper and Row Publishers, Inc. v. Nation Enterprises*, 471 U.S. 539 (1985).

27 *Sony Corporation of America v. Universal City Studios*, 464 U.S. 417 (1984).

28 *Ex parte White*, 66 F Supp 982 (1944).

29 *Schueller v. Drum*, 51 F Supp 383 (1943).

30 *Knox v. Lee*, 12 Wall 457 (1870).

31 *People ex rel Ostwald v. Craver*, 70 NYS 2d 513 (1946).

32 *Kimmelman v. Morrison*, ____U.S.106 sct 2574, 91 L Ed 2d 305 (1986).

33 *State ex rel Warman v. Bushong*, 86 Ohio App 489 (1949).

34 *Zimmerman v. Walker*, 132 F 2d 442 (1942).

35 *Korematsu v. U.S.*, 323 U.S. 214 (1945).

36 *Selective Service System v. Minnesota Public Interest Research Group*, 468 U.S. 841 (1984).

37 *Bowman v. Chicago Ry. Co.*, 125 U.S. 465 (1888).

38 *Bode v. Barrett*, 344 U.S. 583 (1953).

39 *Safe Harbor Water Power Co. v. FPC*, 37 F Supp 9 (1941).

Article Two

1 *Youngstown Sheet and Tube Company v. Sawyer*, 343 U.S. 579 (1952).

26   *Lemon v. Kurtzman*, 403 U.S. 602 (1971).

27   *Committee for Public Education v. Nyquist*, 413 U.S. 756 (1973).

28   *Sloan v. Lemon*, 413 U.S. 825 (1973).

29   *Grand Rapids School District v. Ball*, 473 U.S. 105 sct 3216, 87 L Ed 2d 267 (1986); *Aguilar v. Felton*, 473 U.S. 105 sct 3248, 87 L Ed 2d 290 (1986).

30   *Mueller v. Allen*, 463 U.S. 388 (1983).

31   Higher Education Facilities Act of 1963, 20 U.S.C. ₈ 701 et seq.

32   *Tilton v. Richardson*, 403 U.S. 672 (1971).

33   *Witters v. Washington Department of Services to the Blind*, 474 U.S. 106 sct 748, 88 L Ed 2d 846 (1986).

34   *Widmar v. Vincent*, 454 U.S. 262 (1981).

35   *Dennus v. U.S.*, 341 U.S. 494 (1951).

36   *Taylor v. Mississippi*, 319 U.S. 583 (1943).

37   *McDonald v. Smith*, 472 U.S. 479 (1985).

38   *New York Times Co. v. Sullivan*, 376 U.S. 254 (1964).

39   *Philadelphia Newspapers, Inc. v. Hepps*, 475 U.S. 106 sct 1558, 89 L Ed 2d 783 (1986).

40   *Monitor Patriot Co. v. Roy*, 401 U.S. 265 (1971).

41   *Time, Inc. v. Pape*, 401 U.S. 279 (1971).

42   *Ocala Star-Banner Co. v. Damron*, 401 U.S. 295 (1971).

43   *Dennis v. U.S.*, 341 U.S. 494 (1951).

44   *Bridges v. California*, 314 U.S. 252 (1941).

45   *New York Times Co. v. U.S.; U.S. v. The Washington Post Co.*, 403 U.S. 713 (1971).

46   *Tinker v. Des Moines School District*, 393 U.S. 503 (1969).

47   *Bethel School District v. Fraser*, 478 U.S. 106 sct 925, 89 L Ed 2d 29 (1986).

48   *Board of Education v. Pico*, 457 U.S. 853 (1982).

49   *Papish v. Board of Curators*, 410 U.S. 667 (1973).

50   *Brazenburg v. Hayes*, 408 U.S. 665 (1972).

51   *U.S. v. O'Brien*, 391 U.S. 367 (1968).

52   *Clark v. Committee for Creative Non-Violence*, 468 U.S. 288 (1984).

53   *Spence v. Washington*, 418 U.S. 405 (1974).

54   *Gutknecht v. U.S.*, 396 U.S. 295 (1970).

55   *Breen v. Selective Service*, 396 U.S. 460 (1970).

56   E.g., *Roth v. U.S.*, 354 U.S. 476 (1957); *Accara v. Cloud Books*, 478 U.S. 106 sct 3172, 92 L Ed 2d 568 (1986); *New York v. P.J. Video, Inc.*, U.S. 106 sct 1610, 89 L Ed 2d 871 (1986).

57   *Ginzburg v. U.S.*, 383 U.S. 463 (1966).

58   *Memoirs v. Attorney General of Massachusetts*, 383 U.S. 413 (1966).

59   *Miller v. California*, 413 U.S. 15 (1973).

60   *U.S. v. 37 Photographs*, 402 U.S. 363 (1971).

61   *U.S. v. Reidel*, 402 U.S. 351 (1971).

62   *Mishkin v. New York*, 383 U.S. 502 (1966).

63   *Ginzberg v. New York*, 390 U.S. 629 (1968).

64   *Stanley v. Georgia*, 394 U.S. 557 (1969).

65   *Paris Adult Theaters v. Slaton*, 413 U.S. 49 (1973).

66   *Renton v. Playtime Theaters, Inc.*, ____U.S. 106 sct 925, 89 L Ed 2d 29 (1986).

67   *New York v. Ferber*, 458 U.S. 747 (1982).

68   *National Broadcasting Company v. U.S.*, 319 U.S. 190 (1943).

69   E.g., *Posadas de Puerto Rico Associates v. Tourism Council of Puerto Rico*, 478 U.S. 106 sct 2968, 92 L Ed 2d 266 (1986).

70   *Virginia State Board of Pharmacy v. Virginia Citizens Consumer Council*, 425 U.S. 746 (1976).

71   *Bates v. State Bar of Arizona*, 433 U.S. 350 (1977); *Zauderer v. Office of Disciplinary Counsel of the Supreme Court*, 471 U.S. 626 (1985).

72   *May Stores v. NLRB*, 326 U.S. 376 (1945).

73   *Bachellor v. Maryland*, 397 U.S. 564 (1970).

74   *Flower v. U.S.*, 407 U.S. 197 (1972).

75   *Police Department of Chicago v. Mosley*, 408 U.S. 92 (1972).

76   *Grayned v. Rockford*, 408 U.S. 104 (1972).

77   *Shuttlesworth v. Birmingham*, 394 U.S. 147 (1969).

78   *Cox v. New Hampshire*, 312 U.S. 596 (1941).

79   *Cox v. Louisiana*, 379 U.S. 536 (1965).

80   *Edwards v. South Carolina*, 372 U.S. 229 (1963).

81   *Lloyd Corporation v. Tanner*, 407 U.S. 551 (1972).

82   *Amalgamated Food Employee's Union v. Logan Valley Plaza, Inc.*, 391 U.S. 308 (1968); *Central Hardware Co. v. NLRB*, 407 U.S. 539 (1972).

83   *NAACP v. Alabama*, 357 U.S. 449 (1958).

84   *Healey v. James*, 408 U.S. 169 (1972).

85   *Papish v. Curators*, 410 U.S. 667 (1973).

86   *Federal Election Commission v. National Conservative Political Action Committee*, 470 U.S. 480 (1984).

87   *Kleindeinst v. Mandel*, 408 U.S. 753 (1972).

88   *Immigration and Naturalization Service v. Stevic*, 467 U.S. 407, 81 L Ed 2d 321 (1984).

89   *Immigration and Naturalization Service v. Lopez-Mendoza*, 468 U.S. 1032, (1984).

Second Amendment

1   *U.S. v. Miller*, 307 U.S. 174 (1939).

2   *U.S. v. Warin*, 530 F 2d 106, 1976, *cert den* 426 U.S. 958 (1976).

3   Crime Control and Safe Streets Act, § 1202 (a).

4   *U.S. v. Bass*, 404 U.S. 336 (1971).

5   *Ball v. U.S.*, 470 U.S. 856 (1985).

6   1968 Gun Control Act, 18 U.S.C. § 923.

7   *U.S. v. Biswell*, 406 U.S. 311 (1972).

8   *McMillan v. Pennsylvania*, 477 U.S. 106 sct 2411, 91 L Ed 2d 67 (1986).

Fourth Amendment

1   *Jones v. U.S.*, 357 U.S. 493 (1958).

2   *Stanford v. Texas*, 379 U.S. 476 (1965); *Mapp v. Ohio*, 367 U.S. 643 (1961).

50   *Murphy v. New York Harbor Commission,* 378 U.S. 52 (1964).

51   *Branzburg v. Hayes,* 408 U.S. 665 (1972).

52   *Couch v. U.S.,* 409 U.S. 322 (1973).

53   *McNabb v. U.S.,* 318 U.S. 332 (1943).

54   *Board of Regents v. Ewing,* 474 U.S. 106 sct 507, 88 L Ed 2d 523 (1985).

55   *Youngberg v. Romeo,* 457 U.S. 307 (1982).

56   *Lehr v. Robertson,* 463 U.S. 248 (1983).

57   *Santosky v. Kramer,* 455 U.S. 745 (1982).

58   *Hewitt v. Helms,* 459 U.S. 460 (1983).

59   *Blum v. Yaretsky,* 457 U.S. 991, 73 L Ed 2d 534 (1982).

60   *MacDonald, Sommer and Frates v. Yolo County,* 447 U.S. 106 sct 2561, 91 L Ed 2d 285 (1986).

61   *Planning Commission v. Hamilton Bank,* 473 U.S. 172 (1985).

62   *Hawaii Housing Authority v. Midkiff,* 467 U.S. 229 (1984).

63   *U.S. v. Causby,* 328 U.S. 256 (1946).

Sixth Amendment

1   *Stevenson v. U.S.,* 278 F 2d 278 (1960); *U.S. v. Rojas-Contreras,* ____U.S. 106 sct 541, 88 L E 2d 537 (1985).

2   *Klopfer v. North Carolina,* 386 U.S. 213 (1967).

3   *U.S. v. Ewell,* 383 U.S. 116 (1966).

4   *U.S. v. Hawk,* 474 U.S. 106 sct 648, 88 L Ed 2d 640 (1985).

5   *U.S. v. MacDonald,* 456 U.S. 1 (1982).

6   *Waller v. Georgia,* 467 U.S. 39, (1984); Press-Enterprise Co. v. Superior Court of California, 478 U.S. 106 sct 2735, 92 L Ed 2d 1 (1986).

7   *Press-Enterprise Co. v. Superior Court of California,* 464 U.S. 501 (1984).

8   *Estes v. Texas,* 381 U.S. 532 (1965).

9   *Geise v. U.S.,* 262 F 2d 151 (1958).

10   *Williams v. Florida,* 399 U.S. 78 (1970).

11   *Johnson v. Louisiana,* 406 U.S. 356 (1972).

12   *Ballew v. Georgia,* 435 U.S. 223 (1978).

13   *Apodaca v. Oregon,* 406 U.S. 404 (1972).

14   *Burch v. Louisiana,* 441 U.S. 130 (1979).

15   *Duncan v. Louisiana,* 391 U.S. 145 (1968).

16   *Baldwin v. New York,* 399 U.S. 66 (1970).

17   *Hill v. Texas,* 316 U.S. 400 (1942).

18   *Peters v. Kiff,* 407 U.S. 493 (1972).

19   *Taylor v. Louisiana,* 419 U.S. 522 (1975).

20   *Groppi v. Wisconsin,* 400 U.S. 505 (1971).

21   *Francis v. Franklin,* 471 U.S. 307 (1985).

22   *U.S. v. Bagley,* 473 U.S. 105 sct 3375, 87 L Ed 2d 841 (1985).

23   *Pointer v. Texas,* 380 U.S. 400 (1965); and *Barber v. Page,* 390 U.S. 719 (1968); *Batson v. Kentucky,* 476 U.S. 106 sct 1712, 90 L Ed 2d 269 (1986).

24   *Illinois v. Allen,* 397 U.S. 337 (1970).

25   *Washington v. Texas,* 388 U.S. 14 (1967).

26   *Gideon v. Wainwright,* 372 U.S. 335 (1963).

27   *Escobedo v. Illinois,* 378 U.S. 478 (1964).

28   *Argersinger v. Hamlin,* 407 U.S. 25 (1972).

29   *Mempa v. Rhay,* 389 U.S. 128 (1967).

30   *Specht v. Patterson,* 386 U.S. 605 (1967).

31   *Goldberg v. Kelley,* 397 U.S. 1 (1967).

32   *Evitts v. Lucey,* 469 U.S. 387 (1985); *Strickland v. Washington,* 466 U.S. 668 (1984).

33   *Nix v. Whiteside,* 475 U.S. 106 sct 988, 89 L Ed 2d 126 (1986).

34   *Jones v. Barnes,* 463 U.S. 745 (1983).

35   *McKaskle v. Wiggins,* 465 U.S. 168, 79 L Ed 2d 122 (1984).

36   *Ake v. Oklahoma,* 470 U.S. 68 (1985).

37   42 U.S.C. § 1988.

38   *Blum v. Stenson,* 465 U.S. 886 (1984).

39   *In re Gault,* 387 U.S. 1 (1967).

40   *McKeiver v. Pennsylvania, In re Burris,* 403 U.S. 528 (1971).

41   *In re Winship,* 397 U.S. 358 (1970).

Seventh Amendment

1   *Colgrove v. Battin,* 413 U.S. 149 (1973).

2   *Feres v. U.S.,* 340 U.S. 135 (1950).

3   *Chappell v. Wallace,* 462 U.S. 296 (1963).

Eighth Amendment

1   *Rehman v. California,* 379 U.S. 930 (1964).

2   *Williams v. Illinois,* 399 U.S. 235 (1970); *Tate v. Short,* 401 U.S. 395 (1971); *Beardon v. Georgia,* 461 U.S. 660 (1983).

3   *McDougle v. Maxwell,* 1 Ohio St. 2d 68 (1964).

4   *Whitley v. Albers,* 475 U.S. 106 sct 1078, 89 L Ed 2d 251 (1986).

5   *Solem v. Henry,* 463 U.S. 277 (1983).

6   *Hutto v. Davis,*

7   E.g., *Ramsey v. Ciccone,* 310 F Supp 600 (DC MA 1970); *McCollum v. Mayfield,* 130 F supp 112 (1955); *Hirons v. Patuxent Institution,* 351 F 2d 613 (CCA 4 1965); *Edwards v. Duncan,* 355 F 2d 993 (CCA 4 1966).

8   *Haines v. Kerner,* 404 U.S. 519 (1972).

9   *U.S. v. Muniz,* 374 U.S. 150 (1963).

10   Holder, Angela R., "The Prisoner's Right to Treatment," 216 JAMA 1253, May 17, 1971.

11   *Robinson v. California,* 370 U.S. 660 (1962).

12   *Powell v. Texas,* 392 U.S. 514 (1968).

13   *Specht v. Patterson,* 386 U.S. 605 (1967).

14   *Jackson v. Indiana,* 406 U.S. 715 (1972).

15   *Jones v. U.S.,* 463 U.S. 354 (1983).

16   Holder, Angela R., "The Right to Treatment," 220 *JAMA* 1165, May 22, 1972.

17   *Furman v. Georgia,* 408 U.S. 238 (1972).

49   *Meritor Savings Bank v. Vinson*, 477 U.S. 106 sct 2399, 91 L Ed 2d 49 (1986).

50   *Roberts v. U.S. Jaycees*, 468 U.S. 609 (1984).

51   *Hishon v. King and Spaulding*, 467 U.S. 69 (1984).

52   42 U.S.C. § 2000e at seq.

53   *Grove City College v. Bell*, 465 U.S. 555 (1984).

54   *North Haven Board of Education v. Bell*, 456 U.S. 512 (1982).

55   *Mississippi University for Women v. Hogan*, 458 U.S. 718 (1982).

56   *Reed v. Campbell*, 476 U.S. 106 sct 2234, 90 L Ed 2d 858 (1986).

57   *Gomez v. Perez*, 409 U.S. 535 (1973).

58   *Stanley v. Illinois*, 405 U.S. 645 (1972).

59   *New Jersey Welfare Rights Organization v. Cahill*, 411 U.S. 619 (1973).

60   *Griffin v. Illinois*, 351 U.S. 12 (1956).

61   *Mayer v. Chicago*, 404 U.S. 189 (1971).

62   *Harper v. Virginia State Board of Elections*, 383 U.S. 663 (1966).

63   *Bullock v. Carter*, 405 U.S. 134 (1972).

64   *State v. Alabama Educational Foundation*, 231 Ala 11 (1935).

65   *Kissick v. Garland School District*, 330 SW 2d 708 (1957).

66   *Shapiro v. Thompson*, 394 U.S. 618 (1969).

67   *Graham v. Richardson*, 403 U.S. 365 (1971).

68   *Plyer v. Doe*, 457 U.S. 202 (1982).

69   *Martinez v. Bynum*, 459 U.S. 460 (1983).

70   *San Antonio Independent School District v. Rodriquez*, 411 U.S. 1 (1973).

71   *Vlandis v. Kline*, 412 U.S. 441 (1973).

72   Rehabilitation Act, 20 U.S.C. § 794.

73   *Bowen v. American Hospital Association*, 476 U.S. 106 sct 2101, 90 L Ed 2d 584 (1986).

74   *Alexander v. Choate*, 469 U.S. 287 (1985).

75   Education for All Handicapped Children Act, PL 94-192, 20 U.S.C. § 1401-61.

76   *Irving Township School District v. Tatro*, 468 U.S. 883 (1984); *Board of Education v. Roweley*, 458 U.S. 176, (1982).

77   *Burlington School Committee v. Department of Education*, 471 U.S. 359 (1985).

78   *Lassiter v. Northampton County Election Board*, 360 U.S. 45 (1959).

79   *Davis v. Schnell*, 81 F Supp 872 (DC Ala 1949).

80   1970 Amendments, Voting Rights Act of 1965, 42 U.S.C. § 1973 (aa).

81   *Oregon v. Mitchell*, 400 U.S. 112 (1970).

82   *Baker v. Carr*, 369 U.S. 186 (1962).

83   *Colegrove v. Green*, 328 U.S. 549 (1946).

84   *Georgia v. U.S.*, 411 U.S. 526 (1973); *Karcher v. Daggett*, 462 U.S. 725 (1983); *Thornbrug v. Gingles*, 478 U.S.____, 92 L Ed 2d 25 (1986).

85   *Upham v. Seamon*, 456 U.S. 37 (1982).

86   *Whitcomb v. Chavis*, 403 U.S. 124 (1971); *Mahan v. Howell*, 410 U.S. 315 (1973).

87   *Abate v. Mundt*, 403 U.S. 182 (1971).

88   *Kirkpatrick v. Preisler*, 394 U.S. 526 (1969).

89   *Kramer v. Union Free School District*, 395 U.S. 621 (1969).

90   *Associated Enterprises v. Toltec Watershed Improvement District*, 410 U.S. 43 (1973); *Salyer Land Co. v. Tulare Lake Basin Water Storage District*, 410 U.S. 719 (1973).

91   Civil Rights Act of 1964, 42 U.S.C. § 1981-2000h.

92   *Moose Lodge v. Irvis*, 407 U.S. 163 (1972).

Fifteenth Amendment

1   *Harman v. Forsennius*, 380 U.S. 528 (1965).

2   *Reddix v. Lucky*, 252 F 2d 930 (1958).

3   *Smith v. Allwright*, 321 U.S. 649 (1944).

4   *U.S. v. Manning*, 215 F Supp 272 (1963).

5   Voting Rights Act of 1965, 42 U.S.C. § 1971-74.

6   *South Carolina v. Katzenbach*, 383 U.S. 301 (1966).

7   *Gaston County, North Carolina v. U.S.*, 395 U.S. 285 (1969).

8   Voting Rights Act of 1965, 42 U.S.C. § 1973.

9   1970 Amendments, Voting Rights Act of 1965, 42 U.S.C. § 1973 (aa).

10   *Oregon v. Mitchell*, 400 U.S. 112 (1970).

11   *Georgia v. U.S.*, 411 U.S. 526 (1973).

12   *Hunter v. Underwood*, 471 U.S. 359 (1985).

Twenty-first Amendment

Twenty-fourth Amendment

Twenty-sixth Amendment

Bibliography

General Works

Dawson, Paul A. *American Government Institutions, Policies, and Politics* (Scott, Foresman and Company, 1987).

Devine, Donald J. *The Political Culture of the United States* (Little, Brown, 1972).

Douglas, William O. *An Almanac of Liberty* (Doubleday, 1954).

Dunn, Charles W. *Constitutional Democracy in America: A Reappraisal* (Scott, Foresman and Company, 1987).

Fisher, Louis. *Constitutional Conflicts between Congress and the President* (Princeton University Press, 1985).

Friendly, Fred W. and Martha J. H. Elliott. *The Constitution: That Delicate Balance* (Random House, 1984).

Mendelson, Wallace. *The American Constitution and the Judicial Process* (Dorsey Press, 1980).

Peltason, J. W. *Corwin and Peltason's Understanding the Constitution* (10th ed. Holt, Rhinehart, & Winston, 1985).

Peters, Charles. *How Washington Really Works* (Addison-Wesley, 1980).

Pyle, Christopher H. and Richard Pious. *The President, Congress and the Constitution* (Free Press, 1984).

Robinson, Donald L., ed. *Reforming American Government* (Westview Press, 1985).

Rohr, John A. *To Run a Constitution* (University Press of Kansas, 1986).

Sundquist, James L. *Constitutional Reform and Effective Government* (Brookings Institute, 1986).

Tribe, Laurence. *Constitutional Choices* (Harvard University Press, 1986).

Wilson, Woodrow. *Constitutional Government in the United States* (Reprint, Johns Hopkins University, 1981).

Woll, Peter. *Constitutional Democracy* (2d ed. Little, Brown, 1986).

Introduction and History

Acheson, Patricia C. *The Supreme Court: America's Judicial Heritage* (Dodd, Mead, 1961).

Becker, Carl L. *The Declaration of Independence: A Study in the History of Political Ideas* (Knopf, 1942).

Bowen, Catherine Drinker. *Miracle at Philadelphia* (Little, Brown, 1966).

Dewey, Donald O. *Union and Liberty: A Documentary History of American Constitutionalism* (McGraw-Hill, 1969).

Duker, William F. *A Constitutional History of Habeas Corpus* (Greenwood Press, 1980).

Eidelberg, Paul. *The Philosophy of the American Constitution* (Free Press, 1968).

Farrand, Max. *The Framing of the Constitution* (Yale University Press, 1962).

Fredrich and McClosky. *From the Declaration of Independence to the Constitution* (Bobbs Merrill, 1954).

Jensen, Merrill. *The Making of the American Constitution* (Van Nostrand, 1964).

Ketcham, Ralph. *Presidents Above Party: The First American Presidency 1789-1829* (University of North Carolina Press, 1984).

Kurland, Philip B. and Ralph Lerner. *The Founders' Constitution* (5 vols. University of Chicago Press, 1987).

Kutler, Stanley. *The Supreme Court and the Constitution* (Houghton Mifflin, 1969).

Laslett, Peter, ed. *Locke's Two Treatises of Government* (Cambridge University Press, 1960).

Lewis, Anthony. *The Warren Court: A Critical Evaluation* (Random House, 1969).

McCloskey, Robert. *The American Supreme Court* (Chicago, 1960).

Mitau, G. Theodore. *Decade of Decision: The Supreme Court and the Constitutional Revolution 1954-1964* (Scribners, 1967).

Morison, S. E., H. S. Commager, and W. E. Leuchtenburg. *A Concise History of the American Republic* (Oxford University Press, 1977).

Pleasants, Samuel A. *The Declaration of Independence* (Merrill, 1966).

Pound, Roscoe. *The Formative Era of American Law* (Little, Brown, 1938).

Schwartz, Bernard. *The Reins of Power: A Constitutional History of the United States* (Hill and Wang, 1963).

Smith, David G. *The Convention and the Constitution* (St. Martins, 1965).

Smith, Page. *The Constitution: A Documentary and Narrative History* (William Morrow, 1978).

Storing, Herbert, ed. *The Anti-Federalist: Writings by the Opponents of the Constitution* (University of Chicago Press, 1985).

————. *What the Anti-Federalists Were For* (University of Chicago Press, 1981).

Sutherland, Arthur E. *Constitutionalism in America: Origin and Evolution of Its Fundamental Ideas* (Blaisdell, 1965).

Warren, Charles. *The Making of the Constitution* (Little, Brown, 1929).

Wood, Gordon. *The Creation of the American Republic* (Norton, 1972).

Wright, Benjamin F. *The Growth of American Constitutional Law* (Chicago, 1967).

Casebooks

Barker, Lucius and Twiley W. Barker, Jr. *Civil Liberties and the Constitution Cases and Commentaries* (5th ed. Prentice-Hall, 1985).

Corwin, Edward S. *The Constitution and What It Means To day*, rev. by Harold W. Chase and Craig R. Ducat (14th ed. Princeton University Press, 1978).

Cushman, Robert E. *Leading Constitutional Decisions* (17th ed. Prentice-Hall, 1982).

Goldman, Sheldon. *Constitutional Law* (2d ed. Harper & Row, 1987).

Lockard, Duane and Walter F. Murphy. *Basic Cases in Constitutional Law* (2d ed. Congressional Quarterly Press, 1987).

Rossum, Ralph A. and G. Alan Tarr. *American Constitutional Law* (2d ed. St. Martin's Press, 1983).

Smith, Edward Conrad, ed. *The Constitution of the United States: With Case Summaries* (11th ed. Barnes and Noble, 1979).

Spaeth, Harold J. *The Warren Court: Cases and Commentary* (Chandler, 1966).

Article One—The Congress

Acheson, Dean G. *A Citizen Looks at Congress* (Harper and Row, 1957).

Berman, Daniel M. *A Bill Becomes a Law* (2d ed. Macmillan, 1966).

Davidson, Roger H. and W. J. Oleszek. *Congress and Its Members* (2d ed. Congressional Quarterly Press, 1985).

Dodd, Lawrence C. and B. I. Oppenheimer. *Congress Reconsidered* (3d. ed. Congressional Quarterly Press, 1985).

Edwards, George C. *Presidential Influence in Congress* (W. C. Freeman, 1980).

Fenno, Richard. *Home Style: House Members in Their Districts* (Little, Brown, 1978).

Fiorina, Morris P. *Congress: Keystone of the Washington Establishment* (Yale University Press, 1977).

Fisher, Louis. *Constitutional Conflicts Between Congress and the Presidency* (Princeton University Press, 1985).

Griffith, Ernest S. *Congress: Its Contemporary Role* (New York University Press, 1961).

Jewell, Malcolm E. and Samuel C. Patterson. *The Legislative Process in the United States* (4th ed. Random House, 1986).

Johannes, John R. *To Serve the People: Congress and Constituency Service* (University of Nebraska Press, 1984).

Keefe, William J. and Morris S. Ogul. *The American Legislative Process: Congress and the States* (5th ed. Prentice-Hall, 1981).

Kozak, David C. and J. D. Macartney, eds. *Congress and Public Policy* (2d ed., Dorsey Press, 1987).

Labovitz, John R. *Presidential Impeachment* (Yale University Press, 1978).

LeLoup, Lance T. *Budgetary Politics* (King's Court, 1986).

Miller, James A. *Running in Place: Inside the Senate* (Simon and Schuster, 1986).

Morgan, Donald. *Congress and the Constitution* (Harvard, 1966).

Ogul, Morris S. *Congress Oversees The Bureaucracy: Studies in Legislative Supervision* (University of Pittsburgh Press, 1976).

Oleszek, Walter J. *Congressional Procedures and the Public Process* (Congressional Quarterly Press, 1978).

Polsby, Nelson W. *Congress and the Presidency* (3d ed. Prentice-Hall, 1976).

Redman, Eric. *The Dance of Legislation* (Simon and Schuster, 1973).

Rieselbach, Leroy N. *Congressional Reform* (Congressional Quarterly Press, 1986).

Siff, Ted and Alan Weil. *Ruling Congress* (Penguin, 1977).

Sundquist, James. *The Decline and Resurgence of Congress* (Brookings Institute, 1981).

Volger, David. *The Politics of Congress* (2d ed. Allyn and Bacon, 1977).

Wilson, Woodrow. *Congressional Government* (Meridian Books, 1956).

Wormuth, Francis Dunham and Edwin B. Firmage. *To Chain the Dog of War: The War Power of Congress in History and Law* (Southern Methodist, 1986).

Article Two—The President

Atlantic Council. *The President, The Congress, and Foreign Policy* (University Press of America, 1986).

Barber, James David. *The Presidential Character* (Prentice-Hall, 1977).

Buchanan, Bruce. *The Citizen's Presidency* (Congressional Quarterly Press, 1986).

Burns, James MacGregor. *The Power To Lead: The Crisis of American Presidency* (Simon and Schuster, 1984).

Califano, Joseph, Jr. *A Presidential Nation* (W. W. Norton, 1975).

————. *Governing America* (Simon and Schuster, 1981).

Cannon, Lou. *Reagan* (Putnam, 1982).

Cronin, Thomas E., ed. *Rethinking the Presidency* (Little, Brown, 1982).

————. *The State of the Presidency* (Little, Brown, 1980).

Davis, James M. *The American Presidency* (Harper and Row, 1986).

Edwards, George. *The Public Presidency* (St. Martin's Press, 1983).

Egger, Rowland. *The President of the United States* (McGraw-Hill, 1972).

Fishel, Jeff. *Presidents and Promises* (Congressional Quarterly Press, 1984).

Fisher, Louis. *The Politics of Shared Power* (Congressional Quarterly Press, 1987).

Hargrove, Erwin C. and Michael Nelson. *Presidents, Politics, and Policy* (Random House, 1984).

Hummel, Ralph P. *The Bureaucratic Experience* (St. Martin's Press, 1977).

Kessler, Frank. *The Dilemmas of Presidential Leadership* (Prentice-Hall, 1982).

King, Gary and Lyn Ragsdale. *Vital Statistics on the Presidency* (Congressional Quarterly Press, 1987).

Laski, Harold J. *The American Presidency* (Grosset and Dunlap, 1960).

Leuchtenberg, William E. *In the Shadow of FDR: From Harry Truman to Ronald Reagan* (Cornell University Press, 1985).

Light, Paul C. *The President's Agenda: Domestic Policy Choice from Kennedy to Carter (with Notes on Ronald Reagan)* (Johns Hopkins University Press, 1983).

Lowi, Theodore J., *The Personal President* (Cornell University Press, 1985).

Margolis, Lawrence. *Executive Agreements and Presidential Power in Foreign Policy* (Praeger, 1986).

Mullen, William F. *Presidential Power and Politics* (St. Martin's Press, 1976).

Nathan, Richard. *The Administrative Presidency* (John Wiley, 1983).

Neustadt, Richard E. *Presidential Power* (Wiley, 1980).

Page, Benjamin and M. P. Petrocca. *The American Presidency* (McGraw-Hill, 1983).

Pious, Richard. *The American Presidency* (Basic Books, 1979).

Rockman, Bart A. *The Leadership Question: The Presidency and the American System* (Praeger, 1984).

Schlesinger, Arthur M., Jr. *A Thousand Days: John F. Kennedy in the White House* (Houghton Mifflin, 1965).

_____. *The Imperial Presidency* (Houghton Mifflin, 1973).

Shull, Steve. *Presidential Policy-Making: An Analysis* (King's Court Communications, 1979).

Sorenson, Theodore. *A Different Kind of Presidency: A Proposal for Breaking the Political Deadlock* (Harper and Row, 1984).

Tatalovich, Raymond and Byron Daynes. *Presidential Power in the United States* (Brooks/Cole, 1983).

Thomas, Ann Van Wynen and A. J. Thomas, Jr. *The War Making Powers of the President* (Southern Methodist Press, 1982).

Watson, Richard A. *The Presidential Contest* (John Wiley, 1980).

Watson, Richard A. and Norman Thomas. *The Politics of the Presidency* (2d ed. Congressional Quarterly Press, 1987).

Wayne, Stephen J. *The Legislative Presidency* (Harper and Row, 1978).

White, Theodore H. *The Making of the President 1960* (Atheneum, 1961).

_____. *The Making of the President 1964* (Atheneum, 1965).

_____. *The Making of the President 1968* (Atheneum, 1969).

_____. *The Making of the President 1972* (Atheneum, 1973).

Article Three—The Courts

Abraham, Henry J. *The Judicial Process* (5th ed. Oxford University Press, 1986).

_____. *The Judiciary: The Supreme Court in the Government Process* (6th ed. Allyn and Bacon, 1983).

Baum, Lawrence. *The Supreme Court* (2d ed. Congressional Quarterly Press, 1984).

Blasi, Vincent, ed. *The Burger Court: The Counter Revolution that Wasn't* (Yale University Press, 1983).

Cardozo, Benjamin N. *The Nature of the Judicial Process* (Yale University Press, 1921).

Carp, Robert A. and C. K. Rowland. *Policymaking and Politics in the Federal District Courts* (University of Tennessee Press, 1983).

Carp, Robert A. and Ronald Stidham. *The Federal Courts* (Congressional Quarterly Press, 1985).

Carter, Lief H. *Contemporary Constitutional Lawmaking* (Pergamon Press, 1985).

Cox, Archibald. *The Role of the Supreme Court in American Government* (Oxford University Press, 1976).

Frank, John P. *The Warren Court* (Macmillan, 1964).

Goldman, Sheldon and Thomas P. Jahnige. *The Federal Courts As a Political System* (Harper and Row, 1985).

Jacob, Herbert. *Justice in America: Courts, Lawyers, and the Judicial Process* (3d ed. Little, Brown, 1978).

Jacobsen, Gary J. *The Supreme Court and the Decline of Constitutional Aspiration* (Rowman and Littlefield, 1986).

Magee, James J. *Mr. Justice Black: Absolutist on the Court* (Virginia Legal Studies, 1980).

Miller, Arthur S. *Politics, Democracy and the Supreme Court* (Greenwood, 1985).

Murphy, Walter F. and C. Herman Pritchett. *Courts, Judges, and Politics* (4th ed. Random House, 1986).

Neely, Richard. *How Courts Govern America* (Yale University Press, 1981).

North, Arthur A. *The Supreme Court: Judicial Process and Judicial Politics* (Appleton-Century-Crofts, 1966).

O'Brien, David M. *Storm Center: The Supreme Court in American Politics* (Norton and Company, 1986).

O'Connor, Karen. *Women's Organizations' Use of the Courts* (Lexington Books, 1980).

Posner, Richard A. *The Federal Courts: Crisis and Reform* (Harvard University Press, 1985).

Steamer, Robert. *Leadership and the Supreme Court* (University of South Carolina Press, 1986).

Westin, Alan F. *The Anatomy of a Constitutional Law Case* (Macmillan, 1958).

_____. *The Supreme Court: Views From Inside* (Norton, 1961).

Witt, Elder. *A Different Justice: Reagan and the Supreme Court* (Congressional Quarterly Press, 1986).

Wolfe, Christopher. *The Rise of Modern Judicial Review* (Basic Books, 1986).

Woodward, Bob and S. Armstrong. *The Brethren* (Simon and Schuster, 1979).

Article Four—Interstate Relations

Barton, Weldon V. *Interstate Compacts in the Political Process* (University of North Carolina Press, 1967).

Dilger, Robert J., ed. *American Intergovernmental Relations Today: Perspectives and Controversies* (Prentice-Hall, 1985).

Jackson, Robert H. "Full Faith and Credit: The Lawyers' Clause of the Constitution," (45 *Columbia Law Review* 1 1945).

O'Toole, Laurence J., Jr., ed. *American Intergovernmental Relations* (Congressional Quarterly Press, 1985).

Reynolds, Harry W. *Intergovernmental Relations in the United States* (American Academy of Political and Social Science, 1965).

Virginia Commission on Constitutional Government. *The Full Faith and Credit Clause of the United States Constitution* (1965).

Article Five—Amending the Constitution

Brickfield, Cyril F. *Problems Relating to a Federal Constitutional Convention* (Government Printing Office, 1957).

Freedman, Samuel S. and Pamela J. Naughton. *ERA: May a State Change Its Vote* (Wayne State University Press, 1979).

Grimes, Alan P. *Democracy and Amendments to the Constitution* (Lexington Books, 1978).

Meyers, D. P. *The Process of Constitutional Amendment* (Government Printing Office, 1941).

Article Six—The Supremacy Article and Federalism

Bowman, Ann O. M. and R. C. Kearney. *The Resurgence of the State* (Prentice-Hall, 1986).

Dilgern, Robert J. ed. *American Intergovernmental Relations Today: Perspectives and Controversies* (Prentice-Hall, 1985).

Kilpatrick, James J. *The Sovereign States* (Regnery, 1957).

Riker, William H. *Federalism: Origin, Operation, Significance* (Little, Brown, 1964).

Rockefeller, Nelson A. *The Future of Federalism* (Harvard University Press, 1962).

Stewart, William H. *Concepts of Federalism* (University Press of America, 1984).

Swisher, Carl B. *The Growth of Constitutional Power in the United States* (Chicago University Press, 1946).

Walker, David. *Toward a Functioning Federalism* (Winthrop, 1981).

Wright, Deil S. *Understanding Intergovernmental Relations* (Duxbury, 1978).

Article Seven—Ratification

Elliott, Jonathan. *Debates in the State Conventions* (Lippincott, 1896).

Mason, A. T. *The States Rights Debate: Anti-federalism and the Constitution* (Prentice-Hall, 1964).

Rossiter, Clinton L., ed. *The Federalist Papers* (New American Library, 1961).

———. *The Political Thought of the American Revolution* (Harcourt, Brace & World, 1963).

The Bill of Rights—General Works

Abernathy, M. Glenn. *Civil Liberties under the Constitution.* (University of South Carolina, 1986).

Abraham, Henry J. *Freedom and the Court* (4th ed. Oxford, 1982).

Barker, Lucius and Twiley W. Barker, Jr. *Civil Liberties and the Constitution Cases and Commentaries* (5th Prentice-Hall, 1985).

Brigham, John. *Civil Liberties and American Democracy* (Congressional Quarterly Press, 1984).

Chamberlin, B. F., and C. J. Brown, eds. *The First Amendment Reconsidered* (Longman's, 1982).

Cushman, Robert E. *Leading Constitutional Decisions* (17th ed. Prentice-Hall, 1982).

Douglas, William O. *The Bill of Rights and America* (University of Wichita Press, 1958).

———. *A Living Bill of Rights* (Doubleday, 1961).

———. *The Right of the People* (Doubleday, 1958).

Lipset, S. M. and Earl Raab. *The Politics of Unreason* (University of Chicago Press, 1978).

Morgan, Richard E. *The Law and Politics of Civil Rights and Liberties* (Random House, 1985).

Murray, Charles. *Losing Ground: American Social Policy 1950-1980* (Basic Books, 1984).

Van Alstyne, William W. *Interpretations of the First Amendment* (Duke University Press, 1984).

The First Amendment—Preferred Rights

Religious Freedom

Beggs, David W. *America's Schools and Churches* (Indiana, 1965).

Cord, Robert L. *Separation of Church and State* (Lambeth Press, 1982).

Douglas, William O. *The Bible and the Schools* (Little, Brown, 1966).

Hook, Sidney. *Religion in a Free Society* (University of Nebraska, 1967).

Horwitz, Robert, ed. *The Moral Foundations of the American Republic* (University of Virginia, 1977).

Levy, Leonard W. *The Establishment Clause: Religion and the First Amendment* (Macmillan, 1986).

Lopatto, Paul. *Religion and the Presidential Election* (Praeger, 1985).

Miller, William L. *The First Liberty: Religion and the American Public* (Knopf, 1986).

Muir, William K. *Prayer in the Public Schools* (Chicago, 1967).

Oregon State Bar. *The Flag Salute Cases* (Prentice-Hall, 1968).

Pfeffer, Leo. *Religion, State and the Burger Court* (Prometheus Books, 1984).

Rice, Charles E. *The Supreme Court and Public Prayer* (Fordham, 1964).

Sorauf, Frank J. *The Wall of Separation: The Constitutional Politics of Church and State* (Princeton University Press, 1976).

Viguerie, Richard. *The New Right: We're Ready to Lead* (Caroline House, 1981).

Weber, Paul J. and D. A. Gilbert. *Private Churches and Public Money* (Greenwood Press, 1981).

Wilson, John F. *Church and State in American History* (D. C. Heath, 1965).

Freedom of Speech, Press, and Assembly

Abernathy, Glenn. *The Right of Assembly and Association* (University of South Carolina Press, 1961).

Canavan, Francis. *Freedom of Expression* (North Carolina Academic Press, 1984).

Chafee, Zechariah, Jr. *The Blessings of Liberty* (Lippincott, 1965).

———. *Free Speech in the United States* (Harvard University Press, 1964).

———. *Government and Mass Communications* (University of Chicago Press, 1947).

Clor, Harry M. *Obscenity and Public Morality* (Chicago, 1969).

Commager, Henry S. *Freedom, Loyalty, Dissent* (Oxford, 1954).

DeGrazia, Edward and Roger K. Newman. *Movies, Censors and the First Amendment* (R. R. Bowker, 1983).

Diamond, Edwin. *Telecommunications in Crisis: The First Amendment, Technology and Deregulation* (Cato Institute, 1983).

Emerson, Thomas I. *Toward A General Theory of the First Amendment* (Random House Vintage Books, 1967).

Fortas, Abe. *Concerning Dissent and Civil Disobedience* (World, 1968).

Friendly, Fred W. *Minnesota Rag* (Random House, 1982).

Haiman, Franklyn S. *Speech and Law in a Free Society* (University of Chicago Press, 1981).

Hentoff, Nat. *The First Freedom: The Tumultous History of Free Speech in America* (Delacorte, 1980).

Holmes, Deborah. *Governing the Press* (Westview Press, 1986).

Hudson, Edward G. *Freedom of Speech and the Press* (Public Affairs Press, 1968).

Isaacs, Norman E. *Untended Gates: The Mismanaged Press* (Columbia University Press, 1985).

Krislov, Samuel. *Supreme Court and Political Freedom* (Macmillan, 1968).

Leonard, Thomas C. *Power of the Press* (Oxford University Press, 1986).

O'Brien, David M. *The Public's Right to Know* (Praeger, 1981).

Pritchett, C. H. *The Political Offender and the Warren Court* (Russell, 1959).

Rivers, William. *The Other Government* (Universe Books, 1982).

Rubin, Bernard, ed. *When Information Counts: Grading the Media* (D. C. Heath, 1985).

Shapiro, Martin. *Freedom of Speech: The Supreme Court and Judicial Review* (Prentice-Hall, 1966).

Stevens, John D. *Shaping the First Amendment: The Development of Free Expression* (Sage, 1982).

Van Alstyne, William. *Interpretations of the First Amendment* (Duke University Press, 1984).

The Second Amendment—Firearms

Bakal, Carl. *The Right to Bear Arms* (McGraw-Hill, 1966).

Halbrook, Stephen P. *That Every Man Be Armed: The Evolution of a Constitutional Right* (University of New Mexico Press, 1984).

Kruschke, Earl R. *The Right to Keep and Bear Arms* (Charles C. Thomas, 1985).

The Fourth, Fifth, and Sixth Amendments—Criminal Justice

Ackerman, Bruce. *Private Property and the Constitution* (Yale University Press, 1977).

Baker, Liva. *Miranda: Crime, Law, and Politics* (Atheneum, 1983).

Creamer, J. Shane. *The Law of Arrest, Search and Seizure* (Sanders, 1968).

Dash, Samuel, R. E. Knowleton, and Richard F. Schwartz. *The Eavesdroppers* (Rutgers University Press, 1959).

Feeley, Malcolm M. *The Process is the Punishment* (Russell Sage, 1979).

Friedland, Martin L. *Double Jeopardy* (Oxford, 1969).

Griswold, Erwin N. *The Fifth Amendment Today: Three Speeches* (Harvard University Press, 1955).

Hawkins, Gordon and Franklin E. Zimring, eds. *The Pursuit of Criminal Justice* (University of Chicago Press, 1984).

Hirchel, J. David. *Fourth Amendment Rights* (Lexington, 1979).

Horowitz, Donald. *The Courts and Social Policy* (Brookings Institute, 1977).

Kalven, Harry and H. Zeisel. *The American Jury* (Little, Brown, 1966).

La Fave, Wayne R. *Search and Seizure: A Treatise on the Fourth Amendment* (West Publishing, 1978 and 1984 Supplement).

Lermack, Paul. *Rights on Trial* (Associated Faculty Press, 1983).

Lewis, Anthony. *Gideon's Trumpet* (Random House, 1964).

Medalie, Richard. *From Escobedo to Miranda* (Lerner, 1968).

Michalowski, Raymond. *Order. Law and Crime* (Random House, 1985).

Miller, Leonard G. *Double Jeopardy and the Federal System* (Chicago, 1968).

Murphy, Walter F. *Wiretapping on Trial* (Random House, 1966).

Newman, Donald J. *Introduction to Criminal Justice* (3d ed. Random House, 1986).

Orfield, Lester B. *Criminal Procedure from Arrest to Appeal* (New York University Press, 1947).

Pound, Roscoe. *Criminal Justice in America* (Holt, Rinehart & Winston, 1930).

———. *Justice According to Law* (Yale University Press, 1951).

Seigler, Jay A. *Double Jeopardy* (Cornell University Press, 1969).

Shafer, William J. *Confessions and Statements* (Thomas, 1967).

Silberman, Charles E. *Criminal Violence and Criminal Justice* (Random House, 1978).

Smith, Roger M. *Liberalism and American Constitutional Law* (Harvard University Press, 1985).

Sundquist, James L. *Constitutional Reform and Effective Government* (Brookings Institute, 1986).

Swanson, Charles R., Neil C. Chamelin, and Leonard Territo. *Criminal Investigation* (4th ed. Random House, 1987).

Wilson, James Q. *The Investigators* (Basic Books, 1978).

Wilson, James Q. and Richard Hernstein. *Crime and Human Nature* (Simon and Schuster, 1985).

Wright, Kevin N. *The Great American Crime Myth* (Greenwood Press, 1985).

Younger, Richard D. *The Grandjury in the United States* (Brown University Press, 1963).

The Eighth Amendment—Bail and Punishment

Bedau, Hugo A. *The Death Penalty in America* (3d ed. Oxford University Press, 1982).

Berger, Raoul. *Death Penalties: The Supreme Court's Obstacle Course* (Harvard University Press, 1982).

Bowers, William J. *Legal Homicide: Death as Punishment in America 1864-1982* (Northeastern University Press, 1984).

Goldfarb, Ronald L. *A Critique of the American Bail System* (Harper & Row, 1965).

Meltsner, Michael. *Cruel and Unusual* (Morrow, 1974).

Schwed, Roger F. *Abolition and Capital Punishment* (AMS Press, 1983).

Van den Haag, Ernest and John P. Conard. *The Death Penalty: A Debate* (Plenum, 1983).

The Ninth Amendment—Natural Rights

Ernst, Morris, and Alan Schwartz. *Privacy—The Right to Be Left Alone* (Macmillan, 1962).

Kurland, Philip B. *Some Reflections on Privacy and the Constitution* (Chicago Center for Policy Study, 1976).

O'Brien, David M. *Privacy, Law and Public Policy* (Praeger, 1979).

Patterson, Bennett B. *The Forgotten Ninth Amendment* (Bobbs Merrill, 1955).

Rosenberg, Jerry M. *The Death of Privacy* (Random House, 1969).

Whalen, Charles and Barbara Whalen. *The Longest Debate* (New American Library, 1985).

The Tenth Amendment—State Power

See books on federalism listed under Article Six.

The Twelfth Amendment—The Electoral System

Ceaser, James. *Presidential Selection: Theory and Development* (Princeton University Press, 1979).

Fiorina, Morris P. *Retrospective Voting in American Elections* (Yale University Press, 1981).

Flanigan, William H. and Nancy H. Zingale. *Political Behavior of the American Electorate* (Allyn & Bacon, 1983).

Ginsberg, Benjamin and A. Stone, eds. *Do Elections Matter?* (M. E. Sharpe, 1986).

Mill, John Stuart. *Considerations on Representative Government* (Many editions, 1861).

Nie, Norman, Sidney Verba, and John Petrocik. *The Changing American Voter* (Harvard University Press, 1979).

Peirce, Neal R. and L. Longley. *The People's President: The Electoral College in American History and the Direct-Vote Alternative* (2d ed. Yale University Press, 1981).

Sandoz, Ellis and C. V. Crabb, Jr. *Election 84* (Mentor, 1985).

Wolfinger, Raymond E. and S. J. Rosenstone. *Who Votes?* (Yale University Press, 1980).

The Thirteenth Amendment—Emancipation

Goldwin, Robert A. *100 Years of Emancipation* (Rand McNally, 1965).

McPherson, J. M. *Struggle for Equality* (Princeton University Press, 1964).

The Fourteenth Amendment—Citizenship and Equal Protection of the Laws

Berger, Raoul. *Government by Judiciary: The Transformation of the Fourteenth Amendment* (Harvard University Press, 1977).

Berman, Daniel. *It Is So Ordered; The Supreme Court Rules on School Segregation* (Norton, 1966).

Burnstein, Paul. *Discrimination, Jobs, and Politics: The Struggle for Equal Employment Opportunity in the United States Since the New Deal* (University of Chicago Press, 1985).

Commager, Henry Steele. *The Struggle for Racial Equality* (Harper Torchbooks, 1967).

Cortner, Richard C. *The Supreme Court and The Second Bill of Rights: The Fourteenth Amendment and the Nationalization of Civil Liberties* (University of Wisconsin Press, 1981).

Crain, Robert. *The Politics of School Desegregation* (Doubleday Anchor, 1968).

Curtis, Michael Kent. *No State Shall Abridge: The Fourteenth Amendment and the Bill of Rights* (Duke University Press, 1986).

Edelman, Martin. *Democratic Theories and the Constitution* (State University of New York Press, 1984).

Hochschild, Jennifer L. *The New American Dilemma: Liberal Democracy and School Desegregation* (Yale University Press, 1984).

_____. *What's Fair? American Beliefs About Distributive Justice* (Harvard University Press, 1981).

Kirp, David L. *Just Schools: The Idea of Racial Equality in American Education* (University of California Press, 1982).

Kluger, Richard. *Simple Justice* (Knopf, 1976).

Kritz, Mary M., ed. *U.S. Immigration and Refugee Policy* (Heath, 1982).

Loescher, Gil and J. Scanlan. *Calculated Kindness: Refugees and America's Half-Open Door, 1945-Present* (Free Press, 1986).

McDowell, Garyk L. *Equality and the Constitution* (University of Chicago Press, 1982).

Miller, Loren. *The Petitioners: The Supreme Court and the Negro* (Pantheon, 1966).

O'Neill, Timothy J. *Bakke and Politics of Equality* (Wesleyan University Press, 1984).

Peltason, J. W. *Fifty-eight Lonely Men: Southern Federal Judges and School Desegregation* (Harcourt, Brace and World, 1961).

Schwartz, Bernard. *The School Busing Case and the Supreme Court* (Oxford University Press, 1986).

Sindler, Allen P. *Bakke, DeFunis and Minority Admissions* (Longman, 1978).

Verba, Sidney and G. R. Orren. *Equality in America: The View From The Top* (Harvard University Press, 1985).

Wilkinson, J. Harvie, III. *From Brown To Bakke: The Supreme Court and School Integration: 1954-1978* (Oxford University Press, 1979).

For books on due process of law, see references under Amendments 4-6.

The Fifteenth Amendment—Right to Vote

Forster, Lorn S., ed. *The Voting Rights Act: Consequences and Implications* (Praeger, 1985).

Gillette, William. *The Right to Vote: Politics and the Passage of the Fifteenth Amendment* (Johns Hopkins University Press, 1965).

Jensen, Richard. *The Winning of the Midwest* (University of Chicago, 1971).

Kessel, John. *Presidential Campaign Politics* (Dorsey, 1980).

Maisel, L. Sandy. *Parties and Elections in America: The Electoral Process* (Random House, 1987).

Matthews, John M. *The Legislative and Judicial History of the Fifteenth Amendment* (Johns Hopkins University Press, 1909).

Miller, Warren E. et. al. *American National Election Studies Data Sourcebook, 1954-1978* (Harvard University Press, 1980).

Nie, Norman, Sidney Verba, and John Petrocik. *The Changing American Voter* (Enlarged ed. Harvard University Press, 1979).

Page, Benjamin. *Choices and Echoes in Presidential Elections* (University of Chicago, 1978).

Pomper, George, ed. *The Election of 1984* (Chatham House, 1985).

Smith, Jeffrey A. *American Presidential Elections: Trust and the Rational Voter* (Praeger, 1980).

Wolfinger, Raymond and Steven Rosenstone. *Who Votes?* (Yale University Press, 1980).

The Eighteenth and Twenty-first Amendments—Prohibition and its Repeal

Bordin, Ruth. *Women and Temperance: The Quest for Power and Liberty 1873-1900* (Temple University Press, 1981).

Clark, Norman H. *The Dry Years* (University of Washington Press, 1965).

Dobyns, Fletcher. *The Amazing Story of Repeal* (Willett, Clark, 1940).

Kyvig, David E. *Repealing National Prohibition* (University of Chicago Press, 1979).

Lee, Henry Walsh. *How Dry We Were: Prohibition Revisited* (Prentice-Hall, 1963).

Lyle, John H. *The Dry and Lawless Years* (Prentice-Hall, 1960).

Mertz, Charles. *The Dry Decade* (University of Washington Press, 1969).

The Nineteenth Amendment—Woman Suffrage

DuBois, Ellen C. *Feminism and Suffrage: The Emergence of an Independent Women's Movement in America 1848-1869* (Cornell University Press, 1978).

Gelb, Joyce and Marian Lief Palley. *Women and Public Policies* (Princeton University Press, 1982).

Grimes, Alan P. *The Puritan Ethic and Woman Suffrage* (Oxford University Press, 1967).

Klein, Ethel. *Gender Politics: From Consciousness to Mass Politics* (Harvard University Press, 1984).

Kraditor, Aileen. *The Ideas of the Woman Suffrage Movement* (Columbia University Press, 1965).

Randall, Vicky. *Women and Politics* (St. Martin's Press, 1982).

The Twenty-fourth Amendment—Abolition of the Poll Tax

Ogden, Frederick D. *Poll Tax in the South* (University of Alabama Press, 1958).

Report of the United States Commission of Civil Rights (Government Printing Office, 1959).

The Twenty-fifth Amendment—Presidential Succession

Bayh, Birch. *One Heartbeat Away: Presidential Disability and Succession* (Bobbs-Merrill, 1968).

Committee for Economic Development. *Presidential Succession* (New York, 1965).

Feerick, John D. *The Twenty-fifth Amendment* (Fordham University Press, 1976).

Tompkins, Dorothy L. *Presidential Succession, A Bibliography* (Institute of Governmental Studies, University of California, 1965).

The Twenty-sixth Amendment—Eighteen Year Old Vote

Sigel, Roberta S. and Marilyn B. Hoskin. *The Political Involvement of Adolescents* (Rutgers University Press, 1981).

Index